*For David Huggett, Anglican priest,
missionary statesman, a father-in-God to me
who mentored me in retreat-giving as we led
retreats for Eastern European pastors in
Austria at Schloss Mittersill.*

Endorsements

Judy's story of burnout is a sobering reminder that we do not serve best when we try to do so in our ability without care of self, developing intimacy with Jesus, and being strengthened by him. This book brings together in one place many of God's gifts to people who take time to seek him, rest in him, reflect on his goodness, and remember. It includes many helpful resources, time honored ways to step back and press into Jesus.

Bob Cheatley
President of St. Stephen's University

Pause, Pray and Play is a fruit that comes from a spiritual transformation movement that has deep historical roots in the universal church and is beginning to bloom in new and fresh ways on the Protestant, Evangelical, and Pentecostal branches of the church. In *Pause, Pray and Play*, Judy Davids, out of intense and fruitful ministry as a leader, counselor, and spiritual director, has provided the church with an inspiring, practical, thoughtful, and biblically-based tool to nurture the ancient Christian practice of spiritual transformation in the church today. I highly recommend it to all that want to grow in the practice and experience of spiritual transformation.

Berten A Waggoner
Former National Director of the Association of
Vineyard Churches

Who is this book for? It is for the weary disciple coming to the end of his rope and wanting to do more than simply tie a knot and hang on. It is for the young disciple not wanting to end up burned out and disillusioned. It is for the worn out disciple looking for a way back. It is for the retreat leader looking for a spiritual toolbox. It is for the spiritual leader desiring to create a family or church culture marked by sanity and sacredness. *Pause, Pray, and Play* is written by a spiritual leader who burned out and found God in her brokenness. Judy's journey to wholeness and the lessons learned along the way has helped hundreds of others do the same. I am one of these.

Charles Bello
Author of Prayer as a Place
Senior pastor of Crestwood Vineyard

In *Pause, Pray, and Play: My Story of Burnout and the Lessons I Learned*, Judy Davids provides us with a doable, multifaceted approach to a life of centering on God. She wrote this book out of her own experience augmented with rich resources from classical and contemporary sources on the spiritual disciplines and the contemplative life. Each section is wonderfully applicable to daily life. For example, what Davids writes about "the silent gaze of God" is transformative. I highly recommend *Pause, Pray, and Play* to anyone wanting a deeper life with the Lord, in addition to those who are desperate for rest in the Lord.

Herschel Rosser
Associate pastor at Sugar Land Vineyard

I have just finished reading this excellent presentation of Judy's personal exploration of a journey that people of faith are lovingly called to make by the loving God that has given salvation to the world. Mrs. Davids joyously presents this personal journey into the life of prayer as a gracious invitation that God has given to each of us. It is clear and concise. Judy Davids presents her journey with great humility and with a refreshing authenticity. It also has the quality of being a helpful practical guide on how every Christian can embrace a healthy prayer life, with Sabbath at the center.

She has blessed me with the reaffirmation in my own calling as a Catholic priest for the gift of balance that God wants to give to each of us. Mrs. Davids also uses a healthy mix of resources on the subject of personal prayer, and its practice, which is rooted in what we would call Traditional Catholic Spirituality.

Fr. Chuck Hough III

Acknowledgements

I am so amazed at my great God who has spent most of my life preparing me, refining me, and training me through my own personal burnout experience to lead retreats for pastors. He placed many people in my life that helped Him do this.

My husband, Peter, has been my cheerleader since we met in 1966. He has given me nudges all along the way to do what God has called me to do. His care of our children, his homemaking, and his typing of my papers made it possible for me to complete a masters degree. He continually encouraged me to keep writing on this book, including driving us to Lanier Theological Library or it probably would not have been written.

Pastor and good friend Charles Bello, who attended our second Pastors' Sabbath Retreat (PSR) with his wife Dianna, first challenged me to write this book. He thought that I ought to leave a legacy behind. I am very grateful! He has given permission to include his talks, which were given at the first two Canadian PSRs.

I am so grateful to David Huggett, an Anglican priest and missionary statesman who mentored me in giving retreats for weary, worn, and/or wounded Eastern European pastors at the castle in Mittersill, Austria. He graciously invited me to help him by my praying for the pastoral couples, and we did several retreats together where I learned at Father David Huggett's feet how to give retreats.

I am also grateful to Dr. Patrick Ducklow, psychologist and pastor, and his team of counselors/teachers in Burnaby Counseling Group for their training in Christian counseling. Learning how to listen at the feet of these masters has been invaluable in the ministry that God has called me to.

I am also so grateful to Dr. James Houston, the first Principal of Regent College in Vancouver, British Columbia, for teaching me two courses on prayer and Christian spirituality, for his spiritual direction with me, and for training me how to do spiritual direction with other women. He prayed over me and commissioned me to this work. Dr. Houston also started me on a journey of reading the spiritual classics, reading which I have continued until today, always having a spiritual classic on the go.

The Masters of Christian Studies degree from New College Berkeley was formative in preparing me for this ministry.

Dr. Don Tinder, my church history professor, encouraged me to write a paper on the role of women in ministry in the Plymouth Brethren. This brought freedom to me as I researched in his personal, huge Brethren library and looked at what the Scriptures had to say about women's ministry.

I am forever grateful to Sister Harriet, a Catholic Nun in Regina, Saskatchewan, for giving me spiritual direction for the year of my burnout in 1990. She led me into contemplative prayer, personal retreats, solitude and silence, playing more often, encouraging hobbies and times out with friends. She was a huge help in my recovery process from burnout. She pointed me to God by directing me to stop, rest, listen for that still small voice as Psalm 46:10 says: "Be still and know that I am God."

I am grateful to Ellen Huet, a professional counselor and prayer warrior who spoke to me on the first day I went to the Sugar Land Vineyard. She told me she was encouraged that I had come to Houston. She had been praying for more pastoral care in the church and she saw me as an answer to her prayer. She was a member of our core team in the church, which trained a team of lay counselors and support groups leaders. She was also one of the first people on my American Pastors' Sabbath Retreat team and was on the first Canadian retreat team as well.

The team of lay ministers whom we trained at the Sugar Land Vineyard was thankfully my support community and friends who encouraged me greatly to step forward in the ministry God had called me to do. The team reached the number of 30 before I left, so there are far too many to mention, but you know whom you all were. Praise God for each one of you.

Table of Contents

Introduction:
Three Huge Lessons
Learned through My Burnout

Am I burned out? If so, how badly? What should I do about it? This is the three-part question that I asked the leader of a workshop on burnout in spiritual leaders. I had come to the Christian Association of Psychological Studies (CAPS) Conference in Vancouver, BC, specifically for this preconference workshop at the suggestion of my professor for the reason of asking this question. After calling him and explaining my predicament, my professor and trainer in counseling who sensed that I was burned out and needed to discover how to deal with it, subsequently told me to come to CAPS.

The CAPS workshop leader invited me to book a personal counseling session with him. He listened to my story and answered my questions. Yes, he told me, I was severely burned out, and I needed to take one year off. I needed to stop all counseling and all associated projects. I was stunned at the remedy but relieved by the analysis; for I knew that something was dreadfully wrong with me. It was a relief to have a name for it: a systemic depression called *burnout.*

My symptoms were frequent migraine headaches, lower back pain, an itchy red rash on my skin, an overarching grouchiness and irritability of mood to the point that I had no patience with my children and husband. I had a sour spirit with no compassion for my counseling clients. Put simply, I could not function in my daily life or as a Christian counselor. I could not focus on reading my Bible for it was like reading about dry bones. My prayers seemed to bounce off the ceiling, for God seemed to be a thousand miles away. Someone would come in for counseling, and I would ask myself why in the world this person had come in for counseling since I noticed that I had worse problems than they had. I could no longer respond to a client with a non-anxious healing presence because I was grouchy and irritable all the time, and I was having a hard time covering it up any more. I was in trouble. I wished that people would leave me alone. I had begun to dread answering the telephone, for it might be another counseling client who wanted me to help them, and I was the one who desperately needed help.

My workshop leader was a former Baptist pastor who had personally burned out and had recovered from it. He had since traveled the world giving these workshops to church leaders, discovering that many church leaders were struggling in the same way that he had. He gave all the staggering statistics and described all the symptoms of this state. As I listened to him that day, I began to realize that I had all those same symptoms he had described and that I needed to do something about it *now*.

In my private counseling session, the pastor not only pronounced the diagnosis of severe burnout, as I mentioned above, but also laid out some guidelines for my year off from counseling. He told me not to do it alone but to get a spiritual director with whom to walk through this dark valley. What I needed to do was to *stop*. This included stopping my counseling, stopping all responsibilities in my church, stopping all the leading of groups that I was doing, and getting off the committee to begin a new counseling center, which I had initiated in Regina, Saskatchewan. Only the necessary home and family duties of wife and mother, activities which I could not get out of very easily since my family depended upon me, would continue; but all my professional work-related activities had to stop.

As I flew home to Regina from that conference, I began to count the activities from which I had to resign: five different things. I had to cease involvement in all these activities, find a spiritual director, and go to a medical doctor to see how some of the physical symptoms might be taken care of. I did not know where to begin to find a spiritual director. We did not have such people in our church. When I got home, I asked at the seminary where my husband taught if anyone knew where I could find a spiritual director. They sent me to the Catholics in the city convent, and that is where I found Sister Harriet who agreed to meet with me every Friday morning for the year and give me spiritual direction.

Pray was my first directive from Sister Harriet. She turned me towards contemplative prayer. She suggested that I spend an hour in contemplation every morning. She stopped me from doing my Bible reading. I had been reading a chapter in the Old Testament, a Psalm, and a chapter in the New Testament every morning, a practice that was then very dry and boring for me. She had me begin meditating on Psalm 46:10a: "Be still and know that I am God."

I went away thinking that I could do this, so I began on Monday morning. But I was wrong. I could not sit still and meditate on that verse for an hour. All activity had stopped, and the house was quiet. All my children had left for school, and my husband had left for work, but my mind was going like crazy about every topic under the sun. I was moving like a motion machine inside. I gave up in despair after about 10 minutes. I tried hard to do this every morning all that week but had to go back to Sister Harriet on Friday and tell her that I had failed miserably. After I made my confession, she looked at me and said that she did not realize that I was such a beginner. Her new direction was that I should try it for five to ten minutes per morning during the next week and I could gradually work up to an hour. And, she gave me the following poem and told me to meditate and pray:

A MEDITATION ON PSALM 46:10

Be
do not do
or pretend to be
anything
just be.

Be still
calm those
anxious, unruly
whirling thoughts
into stillness.

Be still and know
as the flower knows the sun's rays
as the heart knows love
open yourselves to knowing.

Be still and know that I am
here and now
around you and within you
behind you and before
wherever you are
I am.

Be still and know that I am God
your Father and Mother
your Companion and Healer
your life and your all.

Be
Be still.
Be still and know.
Be still and know that I am.
Be still and know that I am God.

I went home and began trying to quiet myself and sit still and meditate like it says in Psalm 131:

"Lord, my heart is not proud,
My eyes are not haughty.
I don't concern myself with matters too great
or awesome for me.
But I have stilled and quieted myself,

15

just as a small child is quiet with its mother.
Yes, like a small child is my soul within me.
O, Israel, put your hope in the Lord-
now and always." (NLT)

I was able to meditate consistently for about 10 minutes per day that week. It took me three months to be able to stay quiet for a whole hour. It took me that long to unwind and get the chaos and commotion out of my system. I had actually begun to relax physically as well: my heart and body seemed to go hand in hand. So, when I went in and confidently reported to Sister Harriet that I was able to sit still and meditate for a whole hour every morning, she told me that it was now time for me to go on a retreat, so I made plans to go away to a nearby monastery for five days and do a retreat. I had been meditating on Psalm 46:10 every day for all the days of those three months: *be still.*

I drove to the monastery, checked myself in, unpacked my suitcase, and went into their chapel. No one was around as I knelt in the first pew and began to pray, thanking God for a safe trip and a wonderful place to come and be alone with Him. I stopped and looked up to the front of the chapel, and there on the wall above the altar in one-foot high green letters were the words "Be still, and know that I am God." I was completely undone, for I knew that God had my number. He had uniquely prepared this time and place especially for me. I began to weep as He spoke to me of His special love for me. I knew that He had called me to take this year off and had sent me to Sister Harriet. I knew that He had personally sent me here to be alone with Him.

So, I suddenly knew deep down inside that He loved me in a very special way if He had so carefully prepared all this just for me. With the verses were four beautiful pictures of the grounds around the monastery: one taken in spring, one taken in summer, one taken in fall, and one taken in winter. I basked in God's wonderful presence for about a half hour. Then I bravely went and inquired in the office about the verse behind the altar and discovered that it had been put up about three months before and would soon be taken down. The display was changed with the season. Again, I was simply undone—this was not a coincidence. I knew in my heart with faith that God had had those words put behind that altar just for me, and when I left the monastery, they would be taken down. I was completely overwhelmed that day by God's amazing grace.

I contemplated God's grace and love for me during that whole retreat. He had ordained this time for me to *rest.* I began to see that coming apart with Him was vitally important, for then I could get my own tank filled back up with energy so that I could in turn minister to others. I felt as if God had tucked me away under His wing so that I could be refreshed and so that my perspective could be restored. During my hectic work as a counselor, I had completely lost myself; thus losing my perspective on my marriage, my family life, my counseling, my church, and on God Himself. My spirit had turned sour and my heart had turned bitter and my body was full of pain. Actually, I was in bad shape from any angle from which you might have looked at it. I think that this is the reason my counselor had told me to take a whole year off from everything. It was at this retreat that the concept of Sabbath began to dawn on me. God is really smart—much smarter than me. He had already provided for our need for rest in His institution of Sabbath rest in the dawn of Creation. To recover, I needed an extended Sabbath.

I actually needed a *Sabbath rhythm* of working hard and resting faithfully in my life. I had the working hard bit down pat—I was a workaholic. But I had completely neglected resting for most of my life. I had always been stuck in the "go" mode. A US Marine father who believed in discipline had raised me. I was the eldest child in the family, and "duty" was my middle name. My mother was an adult child of an alcoholic (ACOA) so was a workaholic herself. With this combination, I could not win for losing because I had internalized their ways into my adult lifestyle. My parents had put me in control of my brother and sister when I was only 10 years old, and I had become their substitute parent after school while they both worked. I felt guilty if I rested or did anything to take care of myself. I could hear my mother's voice in the background of my mind, saying, "Get to work, Judy." I had never learned to care for my own needs. I had emotional needs, spiritual needs, physical needs, and mental needs. I had not heeded the flight assistant's instructions in case of emergency to put on your own oxygen mask first and then you can assist others to put theirs on. I could teach others to care for their own needs, but I did not care for myself. I needed to learn how to do my own excellent self-care.

At that first personal retreat, I also fasted for the five days. This spiritual discipline quieted my spirit down a little bit more. I was beginning to slow down and smell the roses. I was slowing down on all levels: physically, mentally, emotionally, and spiritually. Peace was coming in a tangible form to my whole being. In fact, my headaches were gone, the red skin rash had disappeared, and my backache was gone. I had begun to sleep a lot more deeply and better. I even took some naps during the day at this retreat. Napping was not something that I *ever* did at home. Now that I had given myself permission to stop and rest, I found that I could actually fall asleep better than I had been able to before. I stopped feeling so nervous and irritable all the time. I was calmer and more at peace. I had begun to truly and deeply rest.

At the retreat, the spiritual disciplines of solitude and silence also became very important for me. The monks who lived there had a rule of silence, which they faithfully kept. The tremendous peace permeating that place allowed me to be at peace just by being there. It was only there that I began to reflect on the fact that when I'm with people constantly, I do need to periodically withdraw from people to be restored. I needed a rhythm of working and then resting. It is in solitude that the violence of busyness is arrested: the wisdom of dormancy is seen. My energies were being

19

restored in the secret place under His wings. I desperately needed the peace of silence with solitude.

Pray and *rest* were my first two directives. *Play* was the third. I returned from my retreat feeling very refreshed and went back to Sister Harriet and reported my success. She was very pleased with the progress and suggested that I needed to begin working on some hobbies, for I needed to play as well pause and pray. She asked about my hobbies, and I told her that presently I did not have a hobby. "Get one," she said. I went home and began to do my tatting again (making lace with a shuttle and thread), which I had not done in years. I began playing the piano again and singing just for my own pleasure. Then I began to sing to the Lord too. I made a huge garden that spring which brought a lot of life to me. I began a cross-stitching project that I found in a magazine, which had a picture of a little boy and a little girl playing with a kitty. The caption underneath the picture read as follows: "The Lord will bless his people with peace," Psalm 29:11. I stitched a message into my soul while I relaxed even more as my fingers gracefully flew in and out with the needle. I was beginning to play.

I was already a veteran journeyer with my journal, but I began to faithfully journal my recovery progress during my year's sabbatical. This spiritual discipline of journaling was very important to reflect upon three huge questions: Where have I been? Where am I now? And, where am I going? I had lost my perspective and was out of balance; journaling helped me to regain my equilibrium. I worked through my emotional problems and recorded my progress in my journal.

I also took time to begin actively cultivating some personal friendships with people in Regina where we were living at the time. I took a friend out for coffee and simply sat and chatted. I was beginning to get used to not having an agenda—this was certainly new for me. This cultivating of friendships was mandatory for needed support but also to ward off the loneliness and depression, which I was feeling, that comes with too much ministry with no self-care and no play. I needed the support of friendships.

For inspiration, Sister Harriet then turned me towards the classic Catholic writers like Henri Nouwen, Bernard of Clairvaux, Brother Lawrence, and Teresa of Avila. I read Nouwen's *Life of the Beloved*, which helped me see how loved I am by my heavenly Father. I read *The Genesee Diary* and learned how Nouwen had benefited from living in a Trappist Monastery for nine months. I read *The Prodigal Son* and saw how the Father cares for His children. I read a book called *Basking in His Presence* by Bill Volkman, which impacted me to begin to simply bask in my Father's love. As a result, I began to experiment with different prayer models like praying the "prayer of quiet" by simply sitting at Jesus' feet and being quiet and contemplating Him.

One morning as I was doing this, all I could do was cry, so I took this experience back to Sister Harriet and asked her what was going on with me. She said that I was praying the "prayer of tears." As I became quiet in Jesus' presence, the emotion of grief began to surface. I was simply grieving my losses which was a very necessary part of my healing process. I began to read Richard Foster's book *Prayer* and Dallas Willard's books on spiritual disciplines also. The reading of spiritual classics became real food for refueling and recovering. I needed to abide in the Vine of which the Biblical passage in John 15: 1-8 spoke. Because I had become disconnected from my Vine, Jesus, I had begun to wither and die spiritually. So, with the reading of spiritual classics and meditating on the Scriptures, I began to become spiritually alive again. I had begun to refuel and revive.

During my sabbatical, three huge lessons that I had begun to learn surfaced: pause, pray, and play. I needed to put a Sabbath rhythm into my lifestyle, which would enable me to work hard and rest regularly and faithfully, thus being able to venture out into the thick of the battle and conquer the problem or enemy. But then I needed to regularly retreat into a sanctuary for refreshing rest. These three lessons would later become the slogan for the Pastors' Sabbath Retreats, which I would create for weary, worn, and wounded pastors in the American Vineyard Movement. I learned that I needed to practice the spiritual disciplines to keep my own soul invigorated. I learned that I needed hobbies and play in my lifestyle so that I would not become dull and sterile or so that I might prevent burnout from happening again to me. Keeping the Sabbath had brought a healthy balance into my life. I needed to keep the Sabbath holy, as the Lord had commanded me. I learned that I needed to laugh a lot more and enjoy playing with friends; to become like a little child in my heavenly Father's loving arms while I paused, prayed, and played.

Of course, God above all others is our loving support, but I learned that I needed a community of counselors around me to support me in my counseling work. As I listened to my counselor give the workshop on burnout, I learned that I needed to have four out of these seven (I've since added the eighth myself) support systems below in place to safeguard my own mental health:

1. Spouse
2. Extended family
3. Pastor/church family
4. Spiritual Director
5. Counselor
6. Small group of 2-3 trusted friends
7. Peer friend
8. Professional team or work team

I had a spouse and a new pastor with a new church family but no other support because we had just moved to a new city. I was fairly isolated in my professional counseling practice when I burned out. This was one of my big problems; I desperately needed a network of support around me. I was alone and isolated. I learned that to recover from burnout, I had to put a support system in place ensuring that I would not burn out again.

After my sabbatical for recovery, I actually began to counsel again, seventeen months after I had first laid it all down. I remember being so afraid that I had forgotten how to counsel or that I had lost my professional skills. However, what I discovered was that not only did I remember how to counsel but also that I began with much more energy and power because I had been refreshed, revived, and restored from my burned-out state. I was also afraid that I would never build up my clientele again after stopping completely. However, once I had begun again, very slowly with one or two clients, I soon had a full booking of my hours and soon afterwards had a waiting list. There are always hurting people who need help the world over. After my time off, I also got a great job in the first Minirith Meier Clinic to start up in Canada. God was very good to me in supplying work again, and this time it was with a team of counselors in a clinic. I needed not to have worried about these things. I learned the lesson, "Do not worry," for it only takes away from your energy. Pray without ceasing instead.

First, we moved back from Regina to Vancouver. I indeed needed that sabbatical year to be prepared for the next period of my life, which I've entitled "The Year of the Wedding." It began with my husband's parents' 50th wedding anniversary in June 1991. Then we had our 25th wedding anniversary in August of the next summer in 1992. Our eldest daughter had her wedding in September, my parents had their 50th in February, and our middle daughter had her wedding the next June. The Lord knew what was down the road when He ordered me to rest for a year. It was good to take a year off. The rest had restored me to begin again with refreshed vigor, replenished energy, a renewed mind, and restored vision.

After counseling for three more years in the clinic, in our church, and in an additional private practice in my home, my husband and I heard a call to missions and went off to Europe as missionaries. We lived in a castle in Mittersill, Austria, which served as a Retreat Centre and as a Study Centre. I was counselor-in-residence, and my husband was the academic dean for the Study Centre. We had students and retreatants coming from all over Western and Eastern Europe. A retired British Anglican pastor who was a statesman in the Christian Mission Community came to our castle to run retreats for burned out Eastern European pastors. He asked me if I would like to assist him by doing some praying and counseling with these pastors and their spouses. I jumped at the chance to help him with the retreats, which he called "Days of Waiting on God."

We gave three of these retreats together over the next two or three years. This is where I got some mentoring on how to run a retreat for burned out pastors. I listened to his sermons on (1) needing a "Father or Mother in God" for support, (2) the pastor's needing a pastor to shepherd him or her and someone to whom to be accountable, (3) and the pastor's need to go into the desert for spiritual refreshment when his own soul was dry. I learned from the Eastern European pastors what a truly burned out pastor looked like. If I thought that I had been burned out, these pastors were far past being burned out: they were burned to a crisp with only a heap of ashes left. The Holy Spirit taught me how to pray for them and work with them in that state by this wonderful opportunity to discover beauty for ashes and to minister to pastors.

Then my husband and I joined the German-speaking Vineyards in Europe and were on their board, moving from our Castle near Salzburg to an apartment in Innsbruck. I worked for the next three years counseling and teaching German-speaking pastors and their spouses. It was during our time there in Innsbruck, Austria, that Wycliffe Bible Translators invited my husband and me to the Ivory Coast in Africa for their biannual conference. My husband gave the morning Bible devotionals on the Beatitudes and I did over 40 hours of counseling with very tired, worn-out missionaries. Working with Christian leaders who were weary, worn, or wounded in the battle was my training to counsel pastors.

After we had been in Europe as missionaries for six years, I was on holiday visiting my sister in my hometown of Houston, Texas, when I went to visit the Vineyard Church near her. I had seen Vineyards in Europe and in Canada but never in my hometown, and I wanted to know how they had begun. I introduced myself to the pastor and was invited to lunch by him and his wife that day. It was during that lunch hour that I was invited to leave Europe and come work for the American Vineyards helping this pastor who was also the Director of the American Vineyard Denomination to create pastoral care for their pastors in the American

Vineyard. I called my husband who was still in Europe and asked him what he thought of this idea. He said it sounded like God to him. I wished him a Happy 35th Wedding Anniversary as I woke him out of a dead sleep, forgetting as I dialed him, how many hours time change there were from Houston to Innsbruck.

We actually went through a long discernment process but finally came to the conclusion that we were called to go to Houston and work for the Vineyards there, disappointing our German colleagues as we left them and Europe. There was something in store for me that I had never dreamed of before. I had a mission to serve American Vineyard pastors.

So ends my own personal story of burnout and recovery. God did not train me in this way for no reason. He gave me this gift to share: to make it to the finish line doing well, we need to pause, pray, and play! This book will serve as a guide to help you learn the art of each of these skills. The first chapter articulates the need to *pause*. The second through tenth chapters focus on the importance of *prayer* and different models and tools useful in developing that art. The eleventh chapter develops the essential element of *play*. I conclude the book with a final chapter on the importance of community building. I pray your journey is blessed as I share what I have learned on my journey.

Pause: Learning to Stop

Pause. Stopping at regular intervals is the first mandatory part for recovery and prevention of burnout. This stopping was the first event of my own recovery. One needs to stop all work and pause everything periodically; that is, become disentangled from all work and the relationships related to work. This is something that is hard for us to do, for we have these demigod illusions that the world will not turn without us. But it will. Life needs a balanced rhythm and a pattern for living if it is to make any sense to us human creatures. I needed a Sabbath rhythm of working hard but stopping regularly to rest in order to survive and make it to the finish line doing well. And so do you.

As I recovered from my self-inflicted burn out, I learned that others had had this idea of pausing long before me. For example, Saint Benedict wrote a Rule of Life in the sixth century for his monks in a small town near Rome, which is still giving life to many. The Benedictine way of life is credited with the saving of Christian Europe from the ravages of the Dark Ages. The Benedictine Rule incorporated these ideas of a balanced daily rhythm of prayer, study, and work. Jesus talked a lot about the Sabbath in the New Testament, as Moses instituted it in the Old Testament. Then we can go back further to the dawn of creation to watch our Creator at work creating our world during six days and then stopping to rest on the seventh.

Keep the Sabbath Holy

God not only rested on the seventh day after creating our world in the previous six days, but He also consecrated this Sabbath day and called it holy. God modeled for us the rhythm of Sabbath as He spun our world into existence. Then He gave the Law, establishing the Sabbath through Moses to his people, the Jews. We need to copy Him. Look at this portion of Scripture from Hebrews to see what God says about the Sabbath and a rest for the people of God:

> *God's promise of entering his rest still stands, so we ought to tremble with fear that some of you might fail to experience it. For this good news—that God has prepared this rest—has been announced to us just as it was to them. But it did them no good because they didn't believe what God had told them.*
>
> *For only we who believe can enter his rest. As for the others, God said, "In my anger I took an oath: 'They will never enter my place of rest,'" even though this rest has been ready since he made the world. We know it is ready because of the place in the Scriptures where it mentions the seventh day: "On the seventh day God rested from all his work." But in the other passage God said, "They will never enter my place of rest."*
>
> *So God's rest is there for people to enter, but those who first heard this good news failed to enter because they disobeyed God. So God set*

30

another time for entering his rest, and that
time is today. God announced this through
David much later in the words already quoted:

> *"Today when you hear his voice,*
> *don't harden your hearts against him."*

Now if Joshua had succeeded in giving them
this rest in the land of Canaan, God would not
have spoken about another day of rest still to
come. So there is a special Sabbath rest still
waiting for the people of God. For all who have
entered into God's rest have rested from their
labors, just as God did after creating the world.
So let us do our best to enter that rest. But if we
disobey God, as the people of Israel did, we will
fall.

~ Hebrews 4:1-11, NLT

This is our rest: to come to Jesus! He is our rest. But
what on earth does that mean practically? How do we walk
that out: this coming to Jesus to sit at his feet or coming to a
place of rest and peace in our lives? How do we live in his
Shalom (a Hebrew word for peace, wholeness, and well
being)? Granted, as the foundation, we first must come to
Him and surrender to him as the boss of our lives, for He
calls the shots as our Creator and as our Redeemer. This is a
lifestyle attitude of submission to Christ. But what type of
lifestyle do we have as one in His family or in His kingdom?
If we are caught up in the hectic pace of this world, we will
miss His still small voice. We will miss His rest.

Our passage in Hebrews, which talks about entering
God's rest, goes back to Creation and mentions the seventh

31

day or Sabbath Day. It refers to the rhythm that God established in His creation at the dawn of history: to stop all work on every seventh day and rest.

Wayne Muller says the following about Sabbath in his book by that name:

> *In the relentless busyness of modern life, we have lost the rhythm between work and rest. We've lost our sense of SABBATH.*
>
> *SABBATH can refer to a single day of the week. Sabbath can also be a far-reaching, revolutionary tool for cultivating those precious human qualities that grow only in time.*
>
> *SABBATH time—effortless, nourishing rest— can invite a healing of the violence of busyness.*
>
> *SABBATH is a way of being in time where we remember who we are, remember what we know, and taste the gifts of spirit and eternity.*
>
> *SABBATH creates a marker for ourselves so, if we are lost, we can find our way back to our center.*
>
> *SABBATH honors the necessary wisdom of dormancy.*
>
> *SABBATH practice is the practice of taking refuge. Make your home in me, Jesus said, as I make mine in you.*
>
> ~ *Wayne Muller,* Sabbath: Finding Rest, Renewal, and Delight in our Busy Lives

Muller's book has really impacted me with the lost art of keeping the Sabbath. Our American culture has eliminated even our blue laws, which kept stores from opening on Sunday. Young people are penalized if they are not willing to work on Sundays so they could choose to attend church.

An article in *Inc.* magazine written by Margaret Heffernan gives three secrets of the most productive people:

1. They take breaks.

   It's easy to think, as I did, that you will get more done if you never stop. But what's clear is that we can easily get resource depleted (that is tired) and quickly get stuck. Taking a break refreshes your mind, allowing you to see new solutions.

2. They are great collaborators.

   Highly productive people tend to have wide networks. They get more done by bouncing ideas off colleagues, clients, and other contacts.

3. They have lives outside of work.

   Far from being maniacally focused, highly productive people have rich private lives. Interests outside of work hone different skills and let you think in different ways.

~ "The Takeaway," Inc., *June 2012*

The working world norm would have us working 24/7. But, research states in this article above that taking breaks makes one highly productive. Because God knew this, He put a Sabbath rhythm into the universe at the dawn of His creation work, and He commanded us to do this:

> *Observe the Sabbath day, by keeping it holy, as*
> *the Lord your God has commanded you. Six*
> *days you shall labor and do all your work, but*
> *the seventh day is a Sabbath to the Lord your*
> *God.*
>
> *~ Deuteronomy 5: 12-14a, TNIV*

If we take our work seriously, we must also take our rest seriously to survive for the long haul all the way to the finish line still doing well. Working while stretched flat out like I did will only get you burned out, not get more work done or better work done, as I foolishly thought.

Sabbath keeping or having a healthy, balanced rhythm of work and rest is the primary discipline that helps us live within the limits of our humanity and honor Almighty God as our Creator. It is the key to a life lived in tune with the rhythms that God himself interwoven into our world at the dawn of Creation. According to Harold Weiss in his book *Day of Gladness*:

> *Mythologically, the Sabbath is the capstone of*
> *Creation. It consecrates the previous creative*
> *acts and integrates them as God's rest. By*
> *resting on the Sabbath and sanctifying it, God*
> *provided a window into the divine mode of*
> *being. In turn, by resting on the Sabbath,*
> *humans repeat what God did in primordial*
> *time, and this reenactment places humans in*
> *touch with reality. The Sabbath rest of humans*
> *gives to their lives a significance that ordinary*
> *time cannot provide. In this way, the myth*
> *anchors human existence on a transcendent*
> *plane and gives it meaning."*

34

Ongoing Challenge to Sabbath

Even though Sabbath keeping centers us, it seems to be the hardest discipline for us to keep. For instance, I get involved in a project and get so passionately entangled that I think that I can skip the resting part to get it done faster or to accomplish more or to meet the deadline. It was this attitude that caused my personal burnout and complete crash.

Practicing rhythms like working and resting, waking and sleeping, keeping silent and using words, eating and fasting, and being still and being active, helps us learn to wait on God. It doesn't come easily for those of us accustomed to busily trying to make things happen. It takes courage to be restrained, to wait for the work of God in our lives and in the situations we face. I read this wisdom in Ruth Haley Barton's book, *Invitation to Solitude and Silence:*

> *Strangely enough, I have found that the more I am called upon to use words, the more silence I need. The more active leadership or being with people that is required of me, the more solitude I require to maintain my personal balance. Sabbath keeping honors my body's need for regular rest, my spirit's need for periodic refreshment, and my soul's need to find joy and peace again in God's presence. I had to realize my own limitations as a human being and then live within those boundaries. This rhythm is a way to maintain balance and equilibrium in ministry and in life.*

*Learning from the Creation order, we realize
that we are creatures and God is Creator. I have
finite limits of time and space and strength and
energy, but God is infinite. God does not sleep.
He does not have to worry about the aging
process, which slows me down, as I do: He is the
Alpha and Omega, the Eternal One.*

*I am not God. There are limits to my relational,
emotional, mental, and spiritual capacities. God
is the only one who can be all things to all
people. God is the only one who can be in two
places at once. God is the one who never sleeps.
I am not. I need a regular rhythm of rest, a
Sabbath rhythm.*

All too often, we do not honor the sacred Sabbath
rhythm God instituted. We allow the busyness of our lives to
take over, and often we don't realize we have forsaken rest
until we are sidelined by burnout. Even after my recovery
from my burnout in 1990, I still struggle with the pull of
life's activity away from a Sabbath rhythm.

As I prepared for a recent trip, I found myself not
sleeping through the nights the last several days of that last
week. I would wake at 2:00 am and lie there thinking of the
thousand tasks that I had to do the next day. During my
hectic busy days, I found myself being so anxious, to the
point that the anxiety hindered my progress. I panicked
about finishing and getting packed up to leave. So many
activities had consumed our lives. Our daughter, Gwen, and
her husband Brent with their two small boys had surprised
us with a visit over Easter for 10 days. I had written the final

exam for the course I was teaching at St. Stephen's University, administered it, completed all the end of term grading, made out the final grades, and turned them in before going through the activities of the convocation weekend. I attempted to write letters for the Pastors' Sabbath Retreat that would take place in several months. Finally, I packed up to leave for my trip. I was traveling about 120 miles per hour each day, working long hours each day, but I was full of hindering anxiety.

My story likely sounds familiar to most people. Most of us in our culture know only one speed: full steam ahead. And we have been stuck in that speed for a very long time. If we do not establish saner rhythms in our own lives and life patterns that limit our out-of-control activism and contain our compulsive busyness, we will not make it over the long haul. Rather than making the finish line in a healthy manner, many will crumple somewhere along the way in an exhausted heap or simply limp along at a sick pace not doing our job well. We will burn out, become disillusioned, or drop out of the race altogether.

So when we get worn out and perhaps feel like quitting, what do we do? How do we re-create ourselves, regroup, or reorient on the important? We take a rest and stop work from all our labors. Here's a hint: did you notice the "r" words? The answer is *rest*.

Jesus Knew How to Rest

Jesus understood just how quickly our passions, even our most noble, could wear us out if we were not careful. Early in His ministry with the disciples, He began to teach them about the importance of establishing sane rhythms of work and rest.

I've been watching Jesus' actions as I've been reading through the Gospel of Luke. Here are some observations I've made about Jesus' value for rest:

- In Luke 4:1, after His baptism, Scripture says: "Then Jesus, full of the Holy Spirit, left the Jordan River. He was led by the Spirit to go out into the wilderness, where the Devil tempted him for forty days. He ate nothing all that time and was very hungry."
- In Luke 4:42, after healing many people the evening before, the Scripture says of Jesus: "Early the next morning Jesus went out into the wilderness."
- In Luke 5:16, after vast crowds came to hear Him preach and to be healed of their diseases, the Scripture says of Jesus: "But Jesus often withdrew to the wilderness to pray."
- In Luke 6:15 after healing the man with a deformed hand in the Temple and getting into a heated discussion with the Pharisees, the Scripture says of Jesus: "One day soon afterward Jesus went to a mountain to pray, and he prayed

38

to God all night. At daybreak, he called his
disciples to him and chose 12 of them to be
apostles."

Our Lord began His public ministry with a forty-day
fast, and then as He engaged people in ministry, He often
withdrew to the wilderness or to a mountainside to pray.
This is not a secret key but the effective key to Jesus' public
ministry. We must underline it for present-day persons
unless they miss it and skip these times of rest.

Did you know that the average pastor today prays
personally for six minutes per week? I know that you lay
persons who are reading this book are perhaps different
than the average North American pastor; but I do hope that
we are more like Jesus who withdrew often in silence and
solitude to the mountainside to talk with His Father all night
long. Without pauses to pray, talking to our Father to get
direction, or become refreshed after hard work, we cannot
continue to the finish line doing well.

Consider the Alternative

Ruth Haley Barton explains in her book, *Invitation to
Solitude and Silence*:

> *When we continue pushing forward without
> taking adequate time for rest and time for
> prayer, our way of life may seem heroic, but
> there is a frenetic quality to our work that lacks
> true effectiveness. This is because we lose the
> ability to be fully present in the moment—fully
> present to God and fully present to other*

39

people. And we lose the creative ability to discern what is needed in our life or ministry situation.

The result can be "sloppy, panicked desperation," a mental and spiritual state in which we're just trying to get it all done somehow, hanging on only by our fingernails. And this prevents us from the quality of presence that delivers true insight for our situation and faithful, solid friendship in our relationships.

When we are constantly exhausted or depleted, we become overly reliant on urgent voices around us for our direction. We react to symptoms rather than seeking to understand and respond to the underlying causes of the situation. We rely on other people's ideas or the latest trend because we are too tired to listen and observe our own setting and create something uniquely suited for this time and place,

We are blind to the solutions we might have discovered if we had peacefully sat at Jesus' feet like Mary and heard His wisdom out in the wilderness or up on the mountain top. These times of solitude with Him are mandatory, not optional.

Alternatively, when we are rested, we bring steady, alert, and wise attention or mindfulness to our lives. Our actions are characterized by discernment of what is truly needed in our situation. We have the energy and creativity to carry it out well. We are at peace with others and ourselves. When we step outside a lifestyle of rest, we relegate ourselves to depletion.

Creating a Lifestyle of Rest

I often find that people educe a value of the idea of rest, but they simply don't know how to do it, proving that the value is more in concept than actuality. To come to rest, one of the most important things needed is what I've called a *Sabbath rhythm* in our lives. A Sabbath rhythm is the establishment a constant back-and-forth motion between engagement and retreat. We need regular times to engage in the hard battle, giving our best energy to the task of living and working. Then we need regular times to stop and rest when we step back into a sanctuary or haven of protection to gain perspective, re-strategize, re-create our relationships and ourselves, and tend our wounds, an inevitability in the battle of life.

Count the rhythm with me while clapping your hands: 1, 2, 3; 4, 5, 6, SEVEN; or work, work, work, work, work, work; REST. (If you are a musician, this is counted in 6/8 time.) I'm emphasizing the seven to make a point. Count it out loud again, clapping your hands. You could also say, "Go, go, go, go, go, go, STOP!" There needs to be this consistent rhythm in our lives to make it to the finish line doing well.

The challenge for many people is knowing what to do when you stop. This is a time only for you and God, necessitating the disciplines of silence and solitude. You can take an hour a day, an afternoon per week, a day per month, a weekend per season, and a week per year; this will establish a rhythm of Sabbath rest. The concept of Sabbath rest is radically different than vacation time in our US culture. This is time to retreat to a quiet and peaceful sanctuary for rest, a time to be totally alone with God.

I learned during my burnout that I had to do more than just rest to heal from my wounds. I had to develop a lifestyle of rest. It took me much support and time to refine this lifestyle, but I found that seven keys were essential for me to change my lifestyle to find rest (each of the following techniques are described further in later chapters):

1. Maintain a Sabbath rhythm—I must pause, pray, and play.
2. Insert spiritual disciplines into my life to be in a position to grow.
3. Keep a reflective journal, recording God's grace in my life and my gratefulness thereof.
4. Take four or more personal retreats per year, and refocus with a spiritual director each month.
5. Foster a contemplative lifestyle, practicing *lectio divina*, the Examen, and the Prayer of Quiet.
6. Prevent burnout by consciously playing, exercising, cultivating hobbies, and laughing more.
7. Live with support and accountability as part of a community in a small group.

My list is very particular to my unique needs and my weaknesses and flaws as a fallen creature in God's creation. I am an eldest child in my family and have a Type A personality, so I am a workaholic. I use food inappropriately to comfort my loneliness at times. Therefore, I desperately need to take regular retreats and stop working to break the workaholism, and I need the spiritual discipline of fasting to re-orient appropriately with my eating habits. As a result, I've put in place a yearly one-week fasting retreat, which is a must for me.

Keeping a strict Sabbath Rhythm in my life helps to break my workaholism. I need to regularly stop to take a rest. While in Houston, I built into my life a rhythm of four retreats per year with the longer or weeklong one in the spring and a weekend in the other three seasons. Because my life as a counselor is filled with caring for people, I especially need the disciplines of silence and solitude to remain balanced, for being alone with Jesus brings things back into line with His Kingdom and His values. He sets me right side up again after I've been knocked down or beat up out in the world. He also heals my wounds and gives me peace.

The essential element of rest is to place a Sabbath rhythm of "working hard and resting faithfully" into your life. There are many different ways to start, so find what works well for you. You may begin slowly, taking 10 minutes of quiet in the morning before things start racing or at the end of your day. Start today! God's time is now.

The Heart of Spiritual Disciplines

In my personal journey toward developing a Sabbath rhythm, I have found that spiritual disciplines have been a centerpiece to knowing how to rest and knowing what to do during that time of rest. I have learned what spiritual disciplines worked best for me, helping me learn how to rest, regain my health, and help me recreate me and put myself in God's way so that I might grow and experience a deeper intimacy with Him. Many of those disciplines are explored further in the following chapters of this book.

The word *discipline* often carries a negative connotation. Many of us shy away from using this word in relation to our spiritual lives, and as a result we have lost the art of discipline or exercise that draws us closer into God's presence and transformative love. We don't practice spiritual disciplines to become legalistic or mechanical in our relationship with God. Rather, we do these spiritual exercises because, in them, we fall in love with our beloved.

In the year 2000, our family gathered at Christmastime in Innsbruck, Austria, where Peter and I were then living. Our son Ian, aged 20, came and had brought his girlfriend, Buffi. We noticed that he had really changed since the last time we had seen him. He always seemed to want to be in Buffi's presence. If she left the room, he wondered where she had gone. We gave him the option of sleeping on our sofa or sleeping in the building next door, the Innsbruck Vineyard; he chose to sleep on our living room sofa so he could be near Buffi who was sleeping in our spare bedroom. He seemed happy doing anything as long as he was in her presence or as near to her as he could be.

Then we noticed that he had changed his financial priorities. Ian is a worship drummer. When he lived at home with us, he was always browsing in music stores, wanting to buy something for his drum kit or the latest music CD. Now we noticed him stopping at jewelry store windows and looking at diamond rings. He told us about his piggy bank— a jar at home in Vancouver into which he put all his extra change when he came home from shopping or from the university. At Christmas he had $276 in that jar waiting to be added to in order to buy a diamond ring. Then came the April email update to say that $500 was in that jar.

The third thing that we noticed was that he had changed how he used some of his free time. He seemed always to be over at her house. They had begun cooking dinner together in the evenings, going for walks, or going to see a movie. Before, Ian would have trekked to the gym to lift weights or visited his buddy's house to do some programming on his computer.

Fourth, we noticed that he wanted to do everything in his power to make Buffi happy. For instance, he said that he wanted to listen to her because she needed him to do that. He wanted to fulfill her every wish if that were possible. He wanted to change himself so that she would be pleased with him. For instance, he had changed how he dressed and how he combed his hair because she liked him a certain way. He was always staring at her. Once, he looked over at me and asked, "Isn't she beautiful, Mom?" He was always talking about her, describing her good qualities in great detail. He wanted to touch her. It was obvious that she was extremely precious to him.

All these changes had constructed a completely different way of doing life for Ian. Had he worked very hard to make such a drastic turnaround? Did he spend hours practicing or toiling to get his new lifestyle just right? Did he submit himself to hard training and discipline? No! In observing Ian, these changes did not look as if they were hard things for him to do. He seemed very happy in doing these very different behaviors, because they all made Buffi happy and because he was in love with her! He seemed to be walking several feet off the ground, floating rather than struggling and exerting a lot of effort. He smiled constantly, especially when she was near.

Because of our great gratitude that God has prepared a special rest for us, forgiven us, brought us into his family, and given us His peace, we can only fall in love with Him as we come to His Son Jesus and place our trust in Him. It feels like a romance similar to Ian and Buffi's as we change our lifestyle to place ourselves in God's rest and receive His peace for us. This is the heart of spiritual disciplines. Because we love Jesus (and secondarily because we might want to recover from burnout or prevent it and live a balanced life), we need to obediently, purposely, and with personal disciplines in place, learn to pause.

The Spiritual Quest

Every human being is on a spiritual quest whether we recognize it or not. Sometimes we fill this longing with other things than God because we do not recognize His call or are not attentive or aware enough to realize His activity. The God-hole inside us orients the human person toward spiritual wholeness and unity, as Dag Hammarskjold so aptly expresses:

> *Thou takest the pen and the lines dance. Thou takest the flute and the notes shimmer. Thou takest the brush and the colors sing. So all things have meaning and beauty in that space beyond time where Thou art. How, then, can I hold back anything from Thee?*

This sentiment is mirrored in the words of Alphonsus Lliguori, saint and spiritual teacher who lived in the 18th century: "We desire because we have first been desired." In Scripture, we turn to Abraham, who pursued God because God was pursuing him. "I will be your God and you will be my people" (Genesis 17:4-8). The psalmist expressed this idea in the following two verses: "As the deer pants for streams of water, so my soul pants for you, O God. My soul thirsts for God, for the living God. When can I go and meet with God?" (Psalm 42:1-2).

Some of us, like Abraham and the psalmist, are actively seeking God; others of us are actively seeking other ways to fill that "God hole" without realizing their ultimate quest is toward God. Still others live life passively, forfeiting active engagement in their own experiences, tossed about as victims of life's circumstances and the enemy's schemes. We must take action to become actively involved in God's activity in our own lives on that spiritual quest. There are several keys I have learned from classic spirituality to facilitate active engagement with God in our lives: awareness, awakening, solitude and silence, and conversion.

Awareness

To begin this process we must become aware or attentive to the moment, so as not to miss that still small voice. The goal is to become aware of life and learn how not to avoid inactivity but to actually seek it out. This is a concerted mindfulness of the present moment, open to the now. Awareness, mindfulness, and focused attention are all about becoming a disciplined person: the choice to not let life just happen to you but rather to fully participate in the life that you are living. We must therefore make a decision to become aware or alert. Scripture often warns us to be alert.

Awakening

Begin a movement that will lead ever deeper into the spiritual experience. Part of this movement will be the process of recognition, followed by a commitment to learning about the spiritual journey as it has been played out in other people, at different times and places, and sometimes in familiar references and resources, such as the Bible.

The Scriptures are filled with events, experiences, and teaching stories that are intended not only to inspire the reader to respond to the word of God, but also to provide us with insight and direction in our spiritual journey. With the parables, Jesus pushes his audience to see life in a new way, to focus their attention and learn to appreciate the little things in life, to look at the birds in the air, (Luke 12:24), not only to appreciate the little things, but also to learn to step back from the details of life and understand how they are related to the bigger picture, for the birds "neither sow nor reap, they have neither storehouse nor barn, and yet God feeds them." With such straightforward teachings and encouragement, Jesus challenged his audience to learn a simple lesson. In the dynamic proposed, people can understand the necessity of focusing their attention and then stepping back to see how all of life is related and integrated.

This process is simply "waking up," or awakening. The process begins with focused attention and awareness but then goes a step further, recognizing how all of life is related and integrated, or to put it in another way, learning to recognize the "more instead of the less" or see the smaller picture in the context of the bigger picture.

*Spirituality means waking up. Most people,
even though they don't know it, are asleep . . .
They never understand the loveliness and the
beauty of this thing that we call human
existence.*

~ Anthony de Mello, S.J.

*If the inner self is awakened it communicates a
new life to the intelligence where it lives, so
that it becomes a living awareness of itself. And
this awareness, is not something that we have,
but something that we are. It is a new and
indefinable quality of our living being.*

~ Thomas Merton

As we grow in awareness, we must learn the balance of seeking after the first thing: the kingdom of God. Allow me to demonstrate this through my friend's analogy. A rabbit dashed by, swiftly followed by a pack of barking dogs in hot pursuit. Soon after, a second pack of barking dogs barges through the clearing. Not long afterward, that second pack returns home, having given up the chase. They never saw the rabbit; they were only following the barking.

Sometimes a stage of intoxication and arrogance arises with growing awareness, and one has an insatiable thirst to gather knowledge of everything and anything. This may be a distraction from actually finding God. We may be following the barking instead of the rabbit. We should never seek rest or spiritual disciplines as a means unto them selves. They are merely tools that lead to the greatest prize: God. Awareness allows us to see more of God's activity, but the awareness should never cause us to neglect the very One to whom we are being made aware.

Seeking Solitude and Silence

Whenever there is some silence around you, listen to it. That means just notice it. Pay attention to it. Listening to silence awakens the dimension of stillness within yourself, because it is only through stillness that you can be aware of silence.

~ Eckhart Tolle

When the Lord wishes to draw a soul to himself, he leads it into solitude, far from the embarrassment of the world and intercourse with men, and there speaks to it with words of fire. The words of God are said to be of fire, because they melt a soul . . . In fact, they prepare the soul to submit readily to the direction of God.

~ Saint Alphonsus Liguori

Solitude and prayer are the greatest means to acquire virtues. Purifying the mind, they make it possible to see the unseen. Solitude, prayer, love, and abstinence are the four wheels of the vehicle that carries our spirit heavenward.

~ Saint Seraphim of Sarov

A continuing step on the spiritual journey is an experience of the intimate and sacred silence, perhaps coming when you least expect it. God draws you into solitude and silence as you approach closer to Him and leave distractions behind you. God comes in the simple uncluttered moment of silence (1 Kings 19:11-13). Neither wind, nor earthquake, nor a fire represented God; He came in the silence and whispered His message softly to Elijah.

Silence invites us to learn and make the necessary connections in life. Perhaps ultimately, silence is the condition that is necessary in order to become aware of the ultimate truths of life and relationship. It prepares us to enter fully into the relationship with the Other. Silence leads to a way of living life that can best be described as contemplative. Without the experience of contemplation, any experience of God would be incomplete.

Conversion: A Change in Attitude and Perception

The experience of conversion—understood in the spiritual sense as the call to change, repent, or embrace a new way of living—is a dominant theme throughout the Bible. Conversion has everything to do with changing an attitude and perception. To emphasize the action or the activity in a very real sense distracts the person from the core value that could be embraced and enjoyed.

Look at the example of Jesus on the cross in Luke 23:39-43. Even under extreme trauma and immense suffering, He was generous and kind with His last breath. He is teaching His disciples about the generous attitude of the kingdom of God—the converted attitude or changed perspective. This generous attitude permeates our daily choices if we are truly converted.

Conversion is the point where the skills that we have practiced—awareness, awakening, silence, and solitude—all converge. Conversion is the result of becoming aware and awake, of looking at the big picture, resisting the urge to be narrowly focused, convinced of our own limited opinions and judgments. Conversion takes place in the silence and the solitude, the place where we encounter God and where we understand and accept that it is not our way, but God's way. Another story, a parable from the life of Jesus, further illustrates the point.

The owner of a vineyard goes out seeking workers. He adds workers all day long. In the end, he pays each one, the ones beginning early in the morning and also those who came during the last hour the very same wage. "God has a right to be generous." Rejoice in the generosity of God to others and that you can witness it, even when you had to work hard all day long. This is a converted attitude and a kingdom perspective.

In the silence and in the solitude of prayer, through the guidance of the Spirit of God, we are invited into the experience of conversion. Some of our perceptions, attitudes, and judgments will easily be converted while still others, especially those that we might believe define our personalities or which might be of the greatest importance to us, may take a little longer.

A spiritual director or mentor might be very helpful in this process. They can be a person who helps to sustain and encourage you as you learn to see in a new way, to respond to the world around you with a converted attitude of generosity.

> *Earth's crammed with heaven,*
> *And every common bush afire with God;*
> *But only he who sees, takes off his shoes.*
>
> ~ *Elizabeth Barrett Browning*

This quest ends with an experience of life that is grounded in the belief that God is filled with plenty. It is the experience of invitation, encouragement, confidence, gratefulness, and generosity. God's love gives life. His forgiveness generates hope that all will be completed, accomplished, and fulfilled according to His plan. In Jesus' words, we submit to this loving God: "Not what I want but what you want" (Matthew 26:39).

Living the converted life is the abundant life. It brings limitless possibilities. Naomi, rocking her baby grandson, Obed, on her lap had no way of knowing that this babe would be the great, great, great grandfather of Jesus Christ. The experience of all her losses—her husband, her two sons, one daughter-in-law—would lead to this moment of abundance, permeated with promise and hope.

Retreating

Pausing does not come easily to many of us. One way to pause is to incorporate the discipline of retreating into your lifestyle. Actively engaging in retreat can facilitate us on our spiritual quest toward God. Times of extended retreat give us a chance to come home to God's presence and to be open with God in utter privacy about what is true of us. Most importantly, it is a chance to rest in His love. In solitude and silence, I find that the decibel of God's voice goes up in my ears to full volume. This is important for us and for those we serve. It is important to model for those we're bringing up behind us: our families, our spiritual children, and our church family.

I love this definition of retreat taken from Thomas Santa's book *Sacred Refuge: Why and How to Make a Retreat:*

> *Retreat is a renewal for the soul. One makes a personal choice and decision to break away from the normal routines of life and deliberately seek silence, which leads to contemplation, and ultimately to conversion, a new way of seeing and interpreting life from a spiritual perspective . . . Regardless of what may propel a person to seek to incorporate the experience of a retreat into their life, all who make such a decision ultimately are introduced to a process that is life nourishing and even life changing.*

Since some of us are new to retreating, I explain below three types of retreats – using definitions that certain Catholics, who are veteran retreaters, use:

- *A guided retreat*—done with a small group and a spiritual director where most exercises are done in the small group with a director and some are done in solitude and silence. Usually done over a weekend.

- *A directed retreat*—done with a spiritual director but done mostly in solitude and silence. This is traditionally a weeklong retreat where one meets with one's spiritual director for an hour each day.
- *A hermitage retreat*—done totally alone in solitude and silence. Usually done for a week or longer, and sometimes fasting is included in the spiritual exercises.

An example of a typical Catholic directed retreat schedule is as follows:

7:00 am	First formal prayer period
8:15 am	Breakfast in silence
9:15 am	Walking contemplation
10:15 am	Second formal prayer period
11:30 am	Meeting with director
12:30 pm	Lunch, followed by rest and exercise
2:30 pm	Third formal prayer period
3:30 pm	Walking contemplation
5:30 pm	Dinner
7:00 pm	Fourth formal prayer period
8:30 pm	Reflection, journaling, prepare for bed

Vineyard Pastors' Sabbath Retreats that I directed had some structured events in which everyone was encouraged to participate. We have copied the Catholics in some things but done it in our Vineyard, rather relaxed style. Here are the events that all are strongly encouraged to attend.

10:00 am	Worship/teaching
11:30 am	Solitude and silence to reflect and journal—a time for "God and me"
1:00 pm	Lunch
1:30 pm	Free time
6:00 pm	Supper
7:00 pm	Story time with feedback and prayer
9:00 pm	Meditation time/Couple time

Francis de Sales popularized the idea of a personal retreat using the Spiritual Exercises of Saint Ignatius (1567-1622). We will talk about The Examen, one part of the Ignatian Spiritual Exercises, later on.

Types of retreats from a broader perspective:

- Conference or preached retreat—done with a larger group
- Guided retreat—done with a smaller group, directed by a facilitator
- Personal retreat – done by an individual, needing time away in silence and solitude perhaps with a spiritual director.
- Hermitage retreat—done all alone by an individual
- 12-Person retreat—can be done as the first three types above.
- Extended retreat—eight days to 40 days with fasting, if one so chooses.

There are many options available in the choice of retreat center. Find one that meets your personal needs. Prior to your retreat time, set realistic goals and expectations. Retreating is a journey towards intimacy with God and eventual union with Him where His will becomes yours. A retreat director or spiritual director can be very beneficial in helping set goals and expectations and gently guide you on your journey towards the Other. For a greater explanation of the types of retreats, I refer you to Santa's book *Sacred Refuge*, pages 119-124.

Evaluating Your Sabbath Rhythm

Each of these tools can be helpful in facilitating your journey toward a lifestyle incorporating rest. I find it helpful to routinely take an inventory of my Sabbath routine. Take a moment to thoughtfully answer the questions that apply to your situation. Write a journal entry with a Sabbath rhythm plan that includes a personal retreat.

Sabbath Rhythm

- Where is there a Sabbath Rhythm in your life? Is your life balanced?
- Do relationships have a priority place in your life? Is this reflected in your schedule? What do you need to do to change your life to have this priority?
- Has work "for the Lord" taken on an addictive nature and/or replaced your relationship with

the Lord, family, or friends? How can you bring your relationships into the right priority order in your schedule?

- How many times did you stop to pause and play with your spouse and/or children this past month? What do you want to do differently to place a balanced Sabbath rhythm in your life that includes play?
- How strong is your "no" muscle? In what areas do you need to practice it more? With whom do you need to practice it and draw stronger boundaries?

Personal Retreat

- Does the structure of your day incorporate the aspect of a mini personal retreat with spiritual disciplines in it? For instance, is there space in your day when you stop or when you can find some personal peace and bask in His Presence?
- Are there personal retreats in your monthly, quarterly or yearly schedule? What must change to include time apart with the Lord?
- Do you need to request a church budget item for personal retreats for the pastor? (Remember Acts 6:1-6 where deacons were appointed so that the apostles could occupy themselves in prayer and in preaching and in teaching of the Word. How can you apply this principle to your life?)

- Is there time to rest in your life? If not, what will you change to get your proper needed rest?

In concluding the topic of *pause*—stopping, or stepping out of our routine to be drawn into intimacy with God and converted to His way—we set our eyes on the adventure of *prayer*, that place of constant communion with God.

Pause: Identifying Where We Are on the Journey

During my time of burnout, I was forced to pause and then institute rhythms of pause into my life. As I was recovering, God presented me a gift in the form of learning about the spiritual journey of the Christian life. It was a key for me to understand how I had ended up in burnout, what God was presently doing in me, and that He had so much more in store for me.

Up until my burnout, I had been very active, and my Christian journey was primarily an outward journey of service. Then I hit the wall, or stumbled into the "dark night of the soul" as St. John of the Cross, calls it. Though I did not yet have this language, I found myself in a crisis, coming out of stage three and being called into stage four of this journey. I came to learn that we must look at our spiritual maturity as a journey with stages, which I will explore in detail in this chapter.

I first heard of this journey in a seminar led by Dr. Bruce Demarest based on a book, *The Critical Journey*, by Janet Hagberg & Robert Guelich. I could then put a name to what I had experienced. I gleaned additional insights from *When the Heart Waits* by Sue Kidd Monk and *Invitation to a Journey* by Dr. M. Robert Mulholland, Jr.

This explanation of journey can provide framework or context for the process through which God might take us.

This is not to be seen as a detailed road map or "one size fits all" spirituality. It is simply a journey that many of us are taking. It is the one of which I found myself in the middle when I crashed and burned out.

Scripture teaches us that Christian growth, or sanctification as St. Paul calls it, is a developmental process. We all move towards maturity over time. One helpful model of this process is from *The Critical Journey* by Janet Hagberg and Robert Guelich (1995). Their book divides the process into six stages or seasons:

1. The Converted Life (Being)
2. The Learning Life (Knowing)
3. The Active Life (Doing)
   ------ *A TIME OF CRISIS AND CHOICE* ------
4. The Inward Life (Being)
5. The Outward Life (Knowing & Doing)
6. The Life of Love (Being, Knowing, Doing)

The classical Christian journey is a three or four step process:

1. Awakening—initial encounter with God and self, conversion experience
2. Purgation—the bringing of the inner life into harmony with Christ, purging of sin
3. Illumination—deepening relationship with God, a shift from seeing God out there to experiencing God deep within our being
4. Union—the experience of complete oneness with God

This classical 3-4-step model carries similarities to Hagbert and Guelich's and can be seen as integrating into it. Let's explore Hagberg and Guelich's model of the Christian journey more thoroughly. As we explore each of Hagberg and Guelich's stages, I will also integrate the four stages of the classical Christian model, thus utilizing the terminology of both so as to create a clearer depiction of this journey.

A few principles form a foundation upon which we will explore the stages of the journey toward Christian maturity. First, this is a pattern that many, but not all, people experience. Second, the stages are progressive and are all necessary. You can't skip any stage. Third, the stages are not linear or compartmentalized. This means you cannot finish one then check it off forever. God may bring you back to revisit it. We move at different rates through the stages, and may even regress, cycle, or get stuck at a stage. This also means that we may experience a number of stages at the same time, but people tend to have a "home stage" out of which they presently are living. Fourth, God is encouraging us and pushing us to grow, but we retain the ability to resist Him. Consequently, it takes work to grow spiritually towards holiness and maturity in a fallen world. With these principles as the framework for the journey, I will explain each stage more comprehensively.

Stage One: The Converted Life (Being)

During the first stage, we move from darkness to light. We are born again. We often feel humbled, unworthy, or weak in this stage. This is a state of vulnerability, where we begin our journey as pilgrims. God will bring us back to this stage many times to renew and refresh us. The classical model calls this stage *awakening*. Spiritual awakening is a two-sided experience. It is an encounter with the living God; it is also an encounter with our true self. This experience can be a gradual or a radical encounter.

Biblical examples of people who experienced this stage are Zacchaeus (Luke 19:1-10), Lydia (Acts 16:11-15), Saul of Tarsus (Acts 9:1-11), and the return on the Prodigal Son (Luke 15:17-21). Isaiah had an experience of who God is: "I saw the Lord sitting upon a throne, high and lifted up" (Isaiah 6:1). Then in the light of that experience, he awoke to who he was: "Woe is me! I am a man of unclean lips" (Isaiah 6:5). We can be like Jacob, we may be very much aware of who we are as we seek to escape from the mess we have made of our life (Gen 27:41-44). Then we encounter God in the midst of our turmoil: "Surely the Lord is in this place, and I did not know it" (Gen 28:16). Peter, upon seeing the power of Christ exclaimed, "Go away from me, Lord; I am a sinful man" (Luke 5:1-11).

We must be cautious not to remain at this stage. We can stay stuck in "Woe is me; I am sinful and no good" and never have the courage to venture out and take the risk to which God is calling us: walking with Him by faith.

Stage Two: The Learning Life (Knowing)

Sometimes called "the discipled life," this stage is a time of learning and belonging. It is important that we become connected to a local church. Knowledge about God, the Bible, how to live the Christian life, and what to believe become most important to us, and we are often attracted to strong leaders who will teach us.

This can become a very legalistic, black and white stage. We can cultivate an "us against them" mentality. Those who believe like us are good while all others are bad. For example, we may become entrenched in debates such as conservative vs. liberal, home school vs. public school, or evangelical vs. charismatic. This stage is run by shoulds, musts, and oughts.

In this stage, the goal is to know it all and obey it all, in the best sense. Learning, obeying, and belonging express our spirituality. It's a vital stage for growing in skill, knowledge, and devotion. Some biblical examples of people who experienced this Learning Life stage are Timothy under Paul (1, 2 Timothy), Ruth as mentored by Naomi (Ruth), and some of the New Testament Pharisees.

The caution at this stage is to not get stuck in legalism and rules and never break out of this structural prison.

Stage Three: The Active Life (Doing)

This is the "roll up your sleeves and get busy" stage. The focus of our spirituality and faith is working diligently for

God. We are praised for doing that, serving there, or accomplishing such-and-such a task. The emphasis here can be on external things, such as success through converts, programs, attendance, or buildings. Biblical examples include Simon Peter's bold, impulsive leadership (Matt. 26:31-35), Demas (2 Tim. 4:1), and the Prodigal Son's older brother (Luke 15).

In this stage, spiritual maturity is defined as involvement and productivity. Unfortunately, we can do work for God without being close to Him. This can leave us empty, resentful, and exhausted. However, to move on we must face a time of crisis. Sometimes it's easier to stay stuck in the active life than to confront the pain of crisis, so we may get entrenched in this stage without moving further into maturity. In our first decade or so of the Christian walk, we will tend to cycle through the first three stages. The busyness of stage three can be a comfortable mask for the pain of moving forward.

A Time of Crisis and Choice

Between stages three and four lies a time of major crisis. *Purgation* is the classic term used to describe the process of bringing our behavior, attitudes, and desires into harmony with our growing awareness of what the Christian life is all about. This is the place where spiritual disciplines can play an important part in our growth. Purgation within the first three stages of development usually deals with the following areas: renunciation of blatant sins (Gal. 5:19-21), renunciation of willful disobedience, and renunciation of unconscious sins, omissions, and motivations. At this stage God also begins the process of disclosing to us our deep wounds and brokenness in our being in order that we may offer them up to God for healing. God is a consuming fire and will burn out the impurities in our character.

This time of crisis is a time of searching, disappointment, confusion, vulnerability, pain, and uncertainty. It has been called "the wall" or "the dark night of the soul." It may include midlife issues, personal loss, or spiritual burnout. According to many authors, much of the American church is stuck at stage three because staying stuck is easier than facing the pain of this pivotal point in spiritual growth. Furthermore, many of us do not know how to move forward. Activity and productivity are a part of our culture, and going inward seems to be counter-intuitive. Some will decline the invitation to fully surrender control to God. Others will start but feel too alone or afraid and so return to what is familiar. Still others will simply regress to stage one or two, get refreshed, retooled, re-envisioned, and return back to stage three. By God's grace and the movement of the Spirit, many people are able to journey onward to the inward life found in stages four, five, and six.

According to Mulholland, during this time of purgation, God begins dealing with:

> the deep-seated attitudes and inner
> orientations of our being out of which our
> behavior patterns flow. Here purgation deals
> essentially with our "trust structures,"

*especially those deep inner postures of our
being that do not rely on God but on self for our
well-being.*

Many times this happens at midlife, generally
between 35-50 years old. God initiates a "midlife crisis" and
begins to dismantle our false identities and personas that
we have built for ourselves. God begins an intense internal
restructuring.

> *As we attempt to adapt to and protect
> ourselves from the wounds and realities of life,
> we each create a unique variety of defense
> structures—patterns of thinking, behaving, and
> relating designed to protect the ego. These
> egocentric patterns make up our false selves.*
>
> *~ Sue Monk Kidd, When The Heart Waits, p.52*

Those who can work through this phase are liberated
from dependency on manipulative and harmful internal
support systems. To walk through this fire is not to die but
to be transformed and purged. The true self may begin to
immerge. Sue Monk Kidd continues by describing the "dark
night of the soul" in this way:

> *There comes a time when both body and soul
> enter into such a vast darkness that one loses
> light . . . There comes a time when the soul sinks
> down into the night . . . [St. John of the
> Cross] explained that a person may suffer a
> feeling of abandonment by God, as well as
> dryness, emptiness, and a distressing encounter
> with one's own hunger . . . The purpose of the
> dark night is to purge us . . . Previous ways of*

*thinking and relating to God no longer
suffice . . . Merton tells us that the darkness
comes when we allow God to strip away the
false selves and make us into the persons we're
meant to be.*

*Transformation depends on this stripping
away, a process that involves undoing ego
patterns, recasting the old story we created for
ourselves to live in, and unraveling illusions not
only about ourselves but also about God . . . This
stripping away both demands and creates a
temporary darkness."*

~ *Sue Monk Kidd,* When the Heart Waits, *p. 151*

The soul must go into the desert like Jesus did and be
tested and purified. It can also be very disconcerting if we
are not aware of God's activity. I love the manner in which
Teresa of Avila handled this troubling season:

*Teresa of Avila experienced the dark night in a
period of intense opposition and suffering. She
prayed to the Lord, "Why do your treat me so
harshly?" God responded, "This is how I treat
my friends." Teresa replied, "I understand now
why you have so few!"*

~ *Bruce Demarest, Satisfy Your Soul, p.212*

Not everyone's experience with this time of crisis is
the same. For some, it is simply an experience of a midlife
transition; for others it will look more like a midlife crisis.
For those who have learned to process their lives, unpack
their disappointments, and adjust their expectations in a
healthy way, this time will be less traumatic. I believe that if

we can teach people, especially leaders in the first three stages how to develop a contemplative lifestyle, they will go into this stage healthier and better equipped. We may prevent burnout.

Stage Four: The Inward Life (Being)

The journey turns inward at this stage, almost always precipitated by and occurring during a time of crisis. It is a season of surrendering to the love of God. In stage four, we search for inner meaning rather than pat theological answers. We may pull away from Christian activity while seeking God in a more intimate and personal way. It takes a lot of emotional energy to do inner work. Consequently, silence and solitude become important. The energy that went into keeping up your persona can now go into developing the inward life. This stage can be summed up by Isaiah's admonition, "They that wait upon the Lord shall renew their strength. They shall mount up with wings as eagles" (Isaiah 40:31).

To grow here, we must learn to surrender again to the Lord. We must learn to trust Him again, even if we don't see or know where we are going. Often, to grow, we need guidance from a mentor, life coach, or spiritual director—someone who has walked this road ahead of us.

Stage four is characterized as coming to a mature faith and entering the relationship of radical trust in God. As a result, there is a decline of anxiety and an increase of faith. We begin to experience what classical Christian tradition calls detachment. This is a posture consistent with actively turning our whole being over to God so that God's presence, purpose, and power can be released through our lives in all situations. Biblical examples of people in this fourth stage are Elijah after Mt. Carmel (1 Kings 18-19), Simon Peter's confusion/denial/restoration process (Mark 14:66), and the disciples on the Emmaus Road (Luke 24:13-35).

As with each stage, there are dangers in becoming stuck in stage 4. Sometimes we can become "vertical people" who crave solitude and only relate in faith upward towards God. The harm comes when we want to stay still forever and not reach out again and serve others.

Stage Five: The Outward Life (Knowing and Doing)

After the transforming inward journey is launched, Christ directs us outward again during this stage, sometimes referred to as convergence. We reconnect with the active world with a new sense of purpose. This can look like stage three, but the difference is not so much the outer activity but rather the inner motivation. We can seem careless about issues that seemed important earlier, such as creeds, rules, numbers, or production.

During this fifth stage, we study, learn, attend, and serve again—not to gain God's favor or people's approval but out of deep love for God and attachment to Him. We are hungry to fulfill God's purposes for us, and to walk in the good works He has prepared beforehand for us to do. We use our spiritual gifts not out of a sense of duty, but with patience, freshness, and inner calm. We can rest in peace even as we work on those things God has given us to do. Often, a mentor, life coach, or spiritual director is very helpful in our discovering where we are gifted and called to serve. Some examples from Scripture are the Servant (Isaiah 42:1-4), Daniel in the lion's den (Daniel 6), a mature Paul (Acts 13, the Epistles), and a mature Peter (1, 2 Peter).

Stage Six: The Life of Love (Integrating Being, Knowing, and Doing)

In this stage, we act in Christian maturity. Living becomes selfless in love. We can sacrifice for others. We can live like Jesus lived because we are dependent on Him. We can love the unlovely, be kind to the rude, pray for our enemies, and hold our tongue when we are wounded. We worry little about reputation, personal success, things, or comfort. Instead, we desire to spend ourselves for others. We have peace in the midst of struggle, and can do more than we ever thought possible because Christ is made perfect in our weakness. Examples include Jesus (Phil. 2:6-11), the blessed person Jesus speaks of in the Beatitudes (Matthew 5:), and Paul in his love for the Jews (Rom. 9:2). Perhaps Mother Theresa, William Tyndale, Corrie Ten Boom, Henri Nouwen, Hudson Taylor, or Watchman Nee might be good examples as well. Other terms used to describe this stage are *illumination* and *union*. Robert Mulholland, Jr. describes illumination in his book *Invitation to a Journey*:

Illumination is the classical term used to describe the deepening relationship the Christian experiences with God. It is characterized by a radical shift of the deep dynamics of our being, a profound transformation of our relationship with God. Illumination is the experience of total consecration to God in love. Rather than my being in charge of my relationship with God, God is given absolute control of the relationship ... The basic shift in illumination is from seeing God as 'out there' to an experience of God present deep within our being. This goes hand in hand with the deep level of absolute trust to which the purgative stage brings us. As long as God is perceived as "out there," separated from us, we understand ourselves as independent, autonomous beings. We labor under the anxiety that causes us to attempt to retain control of our relationship with God and to control our limited world.

Union is the classical term used to describe an abiding experience of complete oneness with God. Our will, our character, our mission, and our values are the same as Christ's. This union can be both joyful and painful. The purpose and focus of this union is that we would experience the reality of Jesus' prayer "that they also may be in us, so that the world may believe ... so that the world may know that you have sent me" (John 17).

"If all souls developed in cookie-cutter fashion, we would have spirituality by duplication rather than by waiting and transformation. Yet

> *the tendency exists among Christians to want*
> *everybody to be at the same place at the same*
> *time. You know how it goes. Everybody should*
> *be actively ministering. (But even Jesus had*
> *seasons of waiting as well as ministering.)*
> *Everybody should be happy. (But even Jesus*
> *was at times sad, anguished, and in pain.)*
> *Everybody should be relating to God in the*
> *same way. (But even Jesus related to God in*
> *different ways - sometimes inwardly,*
> *sometimes outwardly.) What would happen if*
> *we allowed people to unfurl their wings and*
> *move into the fullness of being each in her own*
> *time and way?"*

~ *Sue Monk Kidd,* When The Heart Waits

Illumination and union do not happen overnight.
While they are a goal to move toward, they cannot be
manufactured and produced by will power alone. We need
the guidance of the Holy Spirit and the love of Christ to enter
this stage. All we can provide is a submitted heart yielded to
God's present activity in our lives in whichever stage we
currently find ourselves. Also, this stage is not like a nirvana
of nothingness. Rather, it is a place of intimate
companionship with God in which He moves within us to do
His will. Like all stages of the journey, we may find that God
has us revisit facets of other stages. We never reach a stage
in which our journey is complete.

It may be helpful at this time to prayerfully examine
your own journey. Take the following questions and journal
the answers to observe your stage of growth:

- What did stage one (the converted life / being) look like for you?
- What did stage two (the learning life / knowing) look like for you?
- What did or does stage three (the active life / doing) look like for you?
- Can you identify cycling through these first three stages a number of times?
- Do you think you are hitting the wall? Why? What does hitting the wall look like for you?
- Do you think you might be at stages four, five, or six? Why?

Pause: Spiritual Disciplines

The journey toward the life of love is not easy, and it doesn't happen spontaneously. We make conscious choices along the journey that bring us further in personal transformation and deeper into relationship with the Father. The spiritual disciplines are a way to actively engage ourselves in this transformative process. Some of the disciplines presented here facilitate pause; others engage us in prayer. This chapter serves as a bridge between the two. Participation in a variety of spiritual disciplines will allow us to keep a Sabbath rhythm and have a balance in our life of pause, pray, and play.

The late Dallas Willard, a respected author and speaker on spiritual disciplines, says the following:

> *The disciplines for the spiritual life are available, concrete activities designed to render bodily beings such as we, ever more sensitive and receptive to the Kingdom of Heaven brought to us in Christ even while living in a world set against God. Lovingly practiced, they join with grace to enable us matter-of-factly "to come boldly to the very throne of God and stay there to receive His mercy and to find grace to help us in time of need." (Hebrews 4:16).*

> *Their wise use allows us to live our lives by this throne of God.*
>
> ~ *Dallas Willard,* The Spirit of the Disciplines

A discipline for the spiritual life, or an exercise unto godliness, is an activity undertaken to bring us into more effective cooperation with Christ and His kingdom. The disciplines are activities undertaken to make us capable of receiving more of God's life and power without harming others or ourselves. Jesus says to each of us personally like he said to Peter, "You follow me!" We each need to make a plan for how to do this in our own lives. I suggest that this plan needs to include a list of the disciplines that fit us in our own situation.

Remember that love is the key in practicing the disciples. Love for Jesus helps us to use the disciplines in our lives without their becoming a new bondage. Spiritual disciplines deepen our union with the heart and mind of God. Love and obedience go together because love alone stays to find a way to obey. Because I love Jesus, His Father will love me, and He will make himself known to me! And their presence will give me light and joy and strength to do all that is right and good. As I center my mind upon His loveliness and kindness, I love him more and more. Recall the story of my son, Ian, and his girlfriend, Buffi. It was not hard for Ian to center his thoughts on his Buffi. She was often his only topic of conversation, undoubtedly his favorite topic of conversation.

Spiritual disciplines have been integral in the lives of believers since the earliest days of the church. Over the centuries, many of these disciplines have withstood the test of time and remain as vital means of connection with God. The following is a list of traditional spiritual disciplines of the church as compiled by Dallas Willard in his book *The Spirit of the Disciplines*. They are divided into two lists: disciplines of abstinence and disciplines of engagement. We will explore each of them more fully.

Disciplines of Abstinence	Disciplines of Engagement
Solitude	Study
Silence	Worship
Fasting	Celebration
Frugality	Service
Chastity	Prayer
Secrecy	Fellowship
Sacrifice	Confession
	Submission

Disciplines of Abstinence

Willard outlines seven disciplines of abstinence. Some of these may look familiar to you because they are keys to rest discussed previously. In our culture of fast-food and credit cards, we often overlook the value of abstaining from things we want. However, disciplines of abstinence create a place of encounter with God and allow Him to meet our every need. The following disciplines each allow us to disengage in activities we would normally involve ourselves in. This type of intentional deprivation allows God opportunities to break into our lives where we didn't realize we were shutting Him out.

Solitude

Solitude is the discipline of purposely abstaining from interaction with other human beings, denying ourselves companionship. It is the primary discipline of abstinence. Solitude allows us to find psychic distance from all people and things. We confront our own soul with its obscure forces and conflicts that escape our attention when we are interacting with others. Choosing to be alone is dwelling on our isolation from other human beings. In stark aloneness it is possible to have silence, to be still and to know Jehovah indeed is God (Psalm 46:10).

Solitude frees us from the mundane daily activities that lock us in. Solitude opens a possibility of a radical relationship to God that can withstand all external events up to and beyond death. I feel free not to be locked into the schedule I keep while living with my husband, in which I cook and we eat at 8:00, 12:30, and 18:00 every day.

One way to practice solitude is by enjoying refreshment in nature, such as by an ocean, river, desert, mountain, or forest. When we lived in British Columbia, I used to retreat on the peninsula of Sechelt in a cabin by the ocean. The very sound of the waves brought peace to my soul as it drowned out all other sounds. The sea gulls flying above gracefully pulled my thoughts upward to God. The majestic evergreens stood stately on the shore to remind me of God's faithfulness.

Solitude is meant to be temporary; it's a time to meet with God, not to escape from people. Practicing the discipline of solitude will pain and threaten our family and friends. I remember taking one retreat and my friend reprimanded me for being so pious and withdrawing from everyone. I was shocked at her words. What she failed to realize is that solitude allows us to reengage in relationships renewed and refreshed. It facilitates authentic relationships with others because we become freer of our hindrances to relationship. It helps us become centered on Christ and remain centered on Him even in the middle of the busyness of our lives after we leave solitude.

Silence

In silence we close off our souls from sounds, whether those sounds be noise, music, or words. Silence goes beyond solitude, and solitude has little effect without it. Silence is the way to make solitude a reality. Silence is frightening because it strips us as nothing else does, throwing us upon the stark realities of our life. Silence reminds us of death, which will cut us off from this world and leave only God and us.

Sound is the last sense to go before death, and it is also one of the first senses we experience. A child can hear in the womb, as I learned when I was pregnant with our son. As I was standing at the bottom of our basement steps, my eight-year-old daughter let go of our metal basement doors, which were too heavy for her, and they slammed shut with a mighty bang. I felt four appendages hit the sides of my womb as my baby within startled at the loud noise, indicating that he had very good ears. So sound bookends our lives.

We also need to practice the abstinence of not speaking. This gives us some inner distance from talking, which helps us to take the time to consider our words more fully.

For me, silence turns up the volume of God's voice somehow by the contrast of cutting out all the other human voices. It also helps me hear my own voice clearly so that I can determine what I think of what God is saying to me. It somehow gives me space and perspective to hear. The supernatural becomes more real for me in the silence.

The purpose of silence and solitude is to slow us down! This frees us from constant interaction with others, rids us of distraction and helps us to gain greater control of the tongue.

Fasting

Fasting is the abstaining in some significant way from food and possibly from drink as well. Quickly we learn a lot about ourselves through this discipline. It can prove humiliating for we will learn how dependent on eating our peace actually is. The pleasure of eating may mask some very unhealthy attitudes in us like low self-esteem or bad attitudes when doing meaningless work or having a lack of rest or exercise. Persons well used to fasting as a systematic practice will have a clear and constant sense of their resources in God. Fasting teaches temperance or self-control and therefore teaches moderation and restraint with regard to all our fundamental drives. Since food has the pervasive place it does in our lives (especially for those in the American culture), the effects of fasting will be diffused throughout our personality.

Fasting confirms our utter dependence upon God by finding in him a source of sustenance beyond food. Fasting is feasting on our Lord. Fasting is a hard discipline to practice because it is all consuming. One needs to do it often enough to become experienced at it, and it also helps to combine it with prayer. Special times of prayer combined with fasting can be a powerful experience. Fasting on Fridays in Lent is a simple way to fast and if one chooses a long fast, one needs to prepare for the fast for a about a week. You would cut down your amount of eating and leave out any addictive substances like caffeine or alcohol. Eating a lot of roughage the day before is helpful to clean out the digestive system. Sometimes taking a laxative on the first night is also helpful in a long fast.

Frugality

Frugality is a discipline defined as abstaining from using money or goods at our disposal in ways that merely gratify our desires or our hunger for status, glamour, or luxury; staying within the bounds of what general good judgment would designate as necessary for the kind of life to which God has led us. In other words, this is living simply instead of frivolously.

The spiritually wise person has always known that frivolous consumption corrupts the soul away from trust in, worship of, and service to God and injures our neighbors as well. Frugality frees us from concern and involvement with a multitude of desires that would make it impossible for us "to do justice, to love mercy, and to walk humbly with our God" (Micah 6:8). We must be free from the bondage that comes from having financial debt (Romans 13:8). Frugality helps us to live out this command.

Chastity

In naming a discipline that deals with sexuality, we do not have a good specific word. Willard chooses chastity to express this spiritual discipline that purposefully turns away from dwelling upon or engaging in the sexual dimension of our relationships to others, even our spouses. Sexuality is one of the most powerful and subtle forces in our human nature, and the percentage of human suffering stemming from it is astounding. As 1 Thessalonians 4:3-4 says: "God wants you to be holy, so you should keep clear of all sexual sin, learning to control your own body and live in holiness and honor-not in lustful passion as the pagans do, in their ignorance of God and his ways."

When we abstain from sex and indulging of sexual feelings and thoughts, we learn how to not be governed by them. Paul says that abstaining from sexual intercourse by mutual agreement in marriage will aid in fasting and praying (1 Corinthians 7:5). Sexuality cannot be allowed to permeate and saturate our lives as it does the life of our culture. Sexuality is at the very core essence of our being as we were created in the image of God.

This discipline is not suggesting no sexuality but instead a proper control and balance of our sexual thoughts, feelings, attitudes, and relations in our life as a whole. By contrast, love and respect for others as persons needs to permeate and saturate our lives as a whole. We could never abuse someone sexually if we love and respect him or her. So, this discipline helps us to curb this natural drive and bring it into proper balance.

Secrecy

Secrecy is a discipline of abstaining from causing our good deeds and qualities to be made known or making our needs made known. This discipline helps us curb the desire for fame, justification, or attention from others. In practicing this discipline, we experience a continuing relationship with God independent of the opinions or thoughts of others. To rise above praise or blame takes great maturity, and this discipline brings this grace into our lives. Jesus tells us that a city set on a hill cannot be hidden (Matthew 5:14).

Good deeds cannot be hidden: Jesus and the disciples could not get away from the crowds. According to Willard, secrecy rightly practiced enables us to place our public relations department entirely in the hands of God. Secrecy teaches love and humility before God and others. When one tells God alone of a need and it is supplied, faith is built. God showed Peter and I the value of this aspect of secrecy one August when we had been crying out to God to help us pay our rent. A church closed on the first of September and sent Peter and I the rest of their money in the bank, and we were able to pay our rent. This was an amazing answer to our secret prayer!

Sacrifice

With the discipline of sacrifice, we abstain from the possession or enjoyment of what is necessary for our living. It is different than frugality in which you abstain from things that are to some degree superfluous anyway. This is total abandonment to God to meet our needs in a supernatural way, and it brings our faith to a higher dimension. Through sacrifice we find that we cannot out-give God! He will always surprise us with his abundance of riches.

Years ago, Peter decided to resign his professorship and step out in faith, move to another province in Canada, and take a position on staff at the Langley Vineyard. That next month we received the largest royalty check for one of his books that he has ever gotten before or since. This check paid for our move, and we lived on it for the next five months until we were able to generate a livable income.

Disciplines of Engagement

Now we turn to the disciplines of engagement. The abstinence disciplines must be counterbalanced with the engagement disciplines. These two are the inbreathing and the out breathing of our spiritual lives and counteract the sins of commission and omission in our souls. It is like carbon dioxide and oxygen in our blood. If the places in our blood designed to carry oxygen are saturated with carbon dioxide, we will die. Abstinence actually breaks the hold of improper engagements in the soul so that God can properly engage it.

Study

With the discipline of study, we engage ourselves with the written and spoken Word of God. This discipline is the chief counterpart of the discipline of solitude; so it is the primary discipline of engagement. Study involves spending time meditating on the parts of the Bible that are important for our spiritual lives combined with constant reading of the Bible as a whole. This might mean sitting regularly under the ministry of gifted teachers. Our aim is to hear God speaking to us through His Word because ultimately the Word of God is God speaking. In other words, we need to meet Jesus, the living Word of God, walking through the pages as we read.

As we study, we might want to use the more concrete method of meditation, which is done by pondering the words of Scripture. Alternatively, we could use the more abstract method of contemplation on one of God's attributes found in the Scripture we are studying. The purpose of our study is increased understanding of God—intellectual and experiential understanding expressed in loving God in our everyday living.

Worship

The study of the word of God opens the way for the disciplines of worship and celebration. Willard states:

In worship we engage ourselves with, dwell upon, and express the greatness, beauty, majesty, and goodness of God through thought and the use of words, rituals, and symbols.

We do this alone as well as in union with God's people. To worship is to see God as worthy, to ascribe great worth to him. We fill our hearts and minds with wonder at the greatness of God. We center on Jesus who is the Lamb of God. We stand in awe of our great God who is worthy of all our praise.

Celebration

Celebration is the discipline that completes worship, for it dwells on the greatness of God as shown in His goodness *to us*. We engage in celebration when we enjoy ourselves, our life, our world, in conjunction with our faith and confidence in God's world as God's work and as God's gift to us. We come together with others who know God to eat and drink, to sing and dance, and to relate stories of God's action for our lives and our people. Miriam, Deborah, and David are good examples of celebrators. Jesus celebrated at the wedding in Cana. With this discipline comes pleasure with balance. We celebrate God's love every Sunday in the Eucharist.

Service

With the discipline of service we engage our goods and strength in the active promotion of the good of others and the causes of God in our world. Not every act of service needs to be a discipline. However, when I serve another to train myself away from arrogance, possessiveness, envy, resentment, or covetousness, it is a discipline for the spiritual life. Service can free us from bondage to other people or from being men pleasers. Serve another as if you were serving the Lord Christ. This is a very important discipline for those who are successful with positions of influence in society. Jesus says that we are to serve others to become great—not be served. We need to strive to serve all people who cross our paths with openness of service to them.

Prayer

Prayer is conversing or communicating with God. When we pray, we talk to God aloud or within our thoughts. The discipline of prayer is often combined with others such as study, meditation, worship, solitude, and/or fasting. Jesus tells us in the Garden of Gethsemane to watch and pray so that we will not enter into temptation. Conversing with God cannot help but have a pervasive and spiritually strengthening effect on all aspects of our personality.

The more we pray, the more we think to pray, and as we see the results of prayer—the responses of our Father to our requests—our confidence in God's power spills over into other areas of our life. Our faith is strengthened. However, prayer as a discipline has its greatest force when we learn to pray without ceasing. We can train ourselves to invoke God's presence in everything that we do. This often requires combining prayer with the disciplines of solitude and fasting to really establish it firmly in our lives.

The purpose of prayer is to align our wills with His will, putting ourselves into a position in which our will yields to His and where it becomes our passion to see His name glorified. Scripture speaks of several types of prayer including intercessory (bringing others before the throne of Grace), praise (adoring our God in prayer), and thanksgiving (simply thanking Him for His love to us). Another form of prayer is contemplative prayer, which is simply sitting in His presence, being with Him and listening to Him. It's simply hanging out with God and will be discussed more in the following chapter.

Fellowship

In the discipline of fellowship, we engage in common activities of worship, study, prayer, celebration, and service with other disciples. This may mean gathering in a large or small group. People united together can maintain more of God and can sustain the force of His greater presence much better than scattered individuals. The coals of a fire can burn much hotter and brighter if all gathered into one spot.

We disciples need contact with each other. We need the gifts of the Spirit that are distributed to the corporate body of Christ all in one place to accomplish a task sometimes. We need each other to be encouraged to keep on keeping on for Christ. I once saw this truth illustrated by a game in the Mittersill Castle. Each person had a candle representing the life of the Christian. Standing together made it hard for Satan to come and snuff out a candle, because a friend beside you could relight it for you. When individuals got separated from the group, Satan had an easy job to blow the candle out and take the person out of the game.

Confession

Confession is a discipline that functions within fellowship. With it we allow trusted others to know our deepest weaknesses and failures. This will nourish our faith in God's provision for our needs through his people, our sense of being loved, and our humility before our brothers and sisters. We let others know who we really are so we do not have to hide or pretend. Confessing helps us to avoid sin because we will receive mercy.

Sharing weaknesses with our Christian community builds bridges in our relationships while sharing strengths builds walls in our relationships. Restitution and reconciliation may naturally follow confession of sin in a mature fellowship. The purpose of confession is to bring sin out into open, exposing ourselves to the truth of God, and allowing Him and others to release us to forgiveness. The purpose of forgiveness is the re-establishment of relationship and this is an opportunity to return into fellowship with God and others.

Submission

The highest level of fellowship—involving humility, complete honesty, transparency, and at times confession and restitution—is sustained by the discipline of submission. In Hebrews 13:7 we read:

> *Obey them that have the rule over you, and submit yourselves: for they watch for your souls, as they that must give account, that they may do it with joy and not with grief.*

The Way of Jesus is mutual submission of all to all (Ephesians 5:21, Philippians 2:3). Submission is a call for help to those recognized as able to give it because of their depth of experience and Christlikeness, because they are truly elders in the Way. Of course this wise person is a servant like Jesus was.

Applying Disciplines to Your Life

The thirteen disciplines described here are some of the main foundational classic disciplines of the spiritual life. There are many others that could be added. You may find others that give you life and facilitate your spiritual growth. We can be very creative here and use our imaginations.

Another way of learning to pray is the discipline of reading Christian books such as biographies of the saints or spiritual classics, which gives us role models to copy. I have devoured books written by Henri Nouwen, Paul Tournier, Dallas Willard, Richard Foster, Larry Crabb, Scott Peck, Walter Wangerin, C. S. Lewis, Teresa of Avila, Brother

Lawrence, Saint Benedict, Madame Guyon, and Saint Francis. I try to keep a classic on-the-go at all times.

Keeping my physical exercise going about six days per week is another secret method of keeping my spiritual disciplines from slipping. The physical and the spiritual seem to go hand-in-hand or seem to work together or be connected somehow for me. I walk in a nearby park for an hour or bicycle on my stationery bicycle in my bedroom for a half hour about five out of seven days. Sometimes I alternate the two since the weather limits being outside at certain times. You will need to find the physical activity that suits you. This is an absolute must for me.

The range or extension of the disciplines is largely determined by our own established tendencies to sin that must be resisted as well as the possible avenues of loving service to God that offer themselves to us. The seven deadly sins listed by the Catholic Church are arrogance, envy, wrath, sloth (laziness), avarice (greed), gluttony, and lasciviousness (lust). We need a rather tough-nosed response to curb our tendency to sin, and the above list of disciplines might just be such a response. When we engage in them conscientiously and creatively and adapt them to our individual needs, time, and place, they help us receive the full Christ-life and become the kind of person that should emerge by following Him.

When Bruce Wilkinson was at a crisis point in his life, he decided to make intimacy with God his top priority, and he made three simple commitments to keep daily:

1. To rise at 5:00 A.M. and read his Bible—read
2. To write one page in a Spiritual Journal—reflect
3. To learn to pray and seek God until he found him—pray.

Perhaps you need to reflect on which disciplines keep you in God's way in order to hear his voice and what it is that will keep you going to finish the race doing well. Each person will have a different list of disciplines, because each of us is a unique creation.

Take some time to draw up a plan for integration of spiritual disciplines, or a Rule of Life. It will help to be mindful of your own personality and sinful tendencies. Confession is not something that I often do naturally. I must seek special ways to do this, and I've found that the best place for me to practice confession is with my spiritual director. Secrecy and submission are hard for me to practice too, because seeking fame or pride is one of my sins. Because I find them awkward, I must actively seek places to practice these three disciplines.

As you develop your own Rule of Life, consider the following questions. What are your strengths and weaknesses? What special disciplines do you need to put in place to help you stay on track? Where is your place of prayer? Consider your situation and your personality with its particular weaknesses and strengths. Tailor your list to your specific needs.

Pray: Communing with God

During my process of recovery after burnout, I began to explore the spiritual disciplines and began to engage in forms of prayer that were new to me. Prayer became an opportunity for me to commune with God. Prayer was no longer something I *did*. Rather, prayer became a *place* I was able to meet with God and be transformed by Him.

A very good friend of mine, Charles Bello, has written a book called *Prayer as a Place* from which many of the ideas and charts in the next few pages come. Charles and his wife, Dianna, came to one of the first Pastors' Sabbath Retreats in the United States that I directed, and they experienced a lot of healing. Charles has gone on to research and write many of his experiences and learnings in several new books. So much healing had been done in their lives that I invited them to come and be part of my team in the first Canadian Pastors' Sabbath Retreat, which I also directed. With Charles' permission, I am incorporating some of his material from those Canadian talks and his book into this chapter.

Charles describes three movements of prayer:

1. **Upward**—worship, praise, adoration, thanksgiving, sacramental prayer, celebration
   Goal: connecting with God (your heart for God)
   Purpose: intimacy
2. **Outward**— intercession, petitioning, praying for the sick and suffering, work

Goal: connecting with God and others (God's heart for others)

Purpose: ministry

3. **Inward**—contemplative

Goal: connecting with God and yourself (God's heart for you)

Purpose: spiritual formation

Prayer has many dimensions. There are many forms of prayer, ways to categorize prayer, and purposes for prayer. We need them all in our lifestyle for we are instructed to pray without ceasing by the Apostle Paul. But this last inward direction of prayer is helpful to transform us more into the likeness of Christ.

Prayer as a Tool for Spiritual Formation

This process of being transformed into the image of Christ has also been called spiritual formation. Paul tells us:

> *And we know that in all things God works for the good of those who love him, who have been called according to his purpose. For those God foreknew he also predestined to be conformed to the likeness of his Son.*

> *~Romans 8:28,29*

This spiritual formation is God's purpose for us. Dr. M. Robert Mullholland Jr. of Asbury Seminary defines Christian spiritual formation in his book, *Invitation to a Journey: A Road Map for Spiritual Formation,* as: (1) a process (2) of being conformed (3) to the image of Christ (4) for the sake of others. To expound on each of these point:

1. **Spiritual formation is a process**—We become a disciple or apprentice of Jesus, and it may take a lifetime to accomplish. We journey daily step by step.

2. **Being conformed**—We will be shaped like Christ to walk like Him, to talk like Him, and to copy Him in the way we live life on every level.

3. **Into the image of Christ**—We will come to look like Him as we journey with Him.

4. **For the sake of others**—We will live our lives loving others and serving others as Christ did on this earth. Our sojourn here on earth will look like His as we compassionately reach out to others like He did.

This is where the spiritual disciplines come into the process. Spiritual disciplines are the primary means of spiritual formation. They are the tools by which we are spiritually formed. Spiritual Disciplines, including prayer, are a place to encounter God. As Martha learned when she complained about Mary's place at Jesus' feet, they are less of an activity and more of a place where we consciously allow ourselves to be in the presence of God. We focus on Him alone and cease our activity. We need to become quiet and still in order to hear Him.

Dallas Willard writes:

> *In disciplines we need to be informed and experimental. They are not righteousness, but wisdom. We must be practical with them, and not picky. We must not be "heroic" or think we are earning anything from God. <u>Disciplines for the spiritual life are places in which we meet Jesus to be taught by him</u>, and he is our guide into how they are best practiced. We should not be overly concerned about how others do them. In a very short time, Jesus will lead us into the practice that is best for us.*

This idea of the disciplines being a place to commune with God is reiterated by Jan Johnson:

> *The purpose of spiritual disciplines is not to change behavior, but to connect our inner motives and needs with God. The effect of that connection is a change of heart.*
>
> *~ Jan Johnson,* When the Soul Listens

So the goal of spiritual disciplines and spiritual formation is not just to change our behaviors; it is to change our heart attitudes. As our hearts are transformed this will naturally change some of our behavior.

To see and experience prayer as a place of personal discovery, let us look at a tool which two psychologists developed called the Johari Window, shown below. This chart illustrates the dynamic between what you see in you and what others see in you. The upper left corner represents what others and you see about yourself. The lower left quadrant represents what you don't allow others to see but you see. What you cannot see yourself but others can see is in the upper right corner. Lastly, the lower right corner represents what no one but God sees; this area is our subconscious or deep inner self.

	What I see	What I don't see
What others see	Public self	Revealed Self (blind spots)
What others don't see	Private self	Hidden Self (subconscious, God's territory)

Our goal in spiritual formation is to become more known by self and others. As we draw close to God, He reveals our deep self to us and then gives us courage to reveal more of ourselves honestly to others, thus the arrow goes from our subconscious to our private self in the chart below, indicating growth. As we become more and more transparent, we become more healthy, whole and integrated. This is one of the great benefits of spiritual disciplines, especially contemplative prayer, which I will explain over the next few pages.

Take this chart below and look at the fours windows and reflect on yourself. Prayerfully answer the questions below the chart to discover more about yourself. This exercise can be done periodically to walk forward in this process of discovery.

1. What does your public self look like? Describe how you want to be perceived by others.
2. What does your private self look like? Describe what you feel a need to hide from others.
3. What do others say are your blind spots (revealed self)?
4. What parts of your unknown self has God revealed to you in the past? How has He revealed it? What are some of the issues He is speaking to in the present?

Contemplative Prayer

One form of prayer I discovered that greatly facilitated spiritual formation was contemplative prayer. Contemplative prayer was one of the first things that began my healing journey in 1990 when I burned out. My spiritual director began instructing me in this method of prayer and set me to practicing it. As I disclosed earlier, it took me three months to calm my mind down or become still inside so that I could contemplate for an hour. It was a learning process, which came step by step as I kept trying to follow the directions of my spiritual director. She had me use a phrase from a scripture verse, "Be still and know that I am God," to accomplish this quieting down of my soul. This repetition of that scripture is an example of contemplative prayer.

Since that time I have read the manual on contemplation from the World Community for Christian Meditation by Benedictine Monk and priest John Main. He talks about this prayer of the heart as a way of simplicity, silence, and stillness. He has done a lot to revive this Christian discipline, which had been set aside and seen as heretical in some cases by western Christianity. He quotes John Cassian, a desert monastic Christian, who says that when seeking to learn this skill, "experience is the teacher."

How to Practice Contemplative Prayer

Before beginning contemplative prayer, find a quiet place alone. Close the door if needed to prevent distraction. As you sit, close your eyes lightly, relax, and breathe deeply. You could light a candle or place a cross on a small table in front of you to prepare the atmosphere in the room. Pick a prayer word to gently say in your mind over and over as you focus on your breathing. Fr. John Mains suggests using the Greek word *maranatha* which means "Lord Jesus come." I simply use the Lord's name, Jesus. Repeat this prayer word to yourself every time your mind wanders. Come in a loving, worshipful, adoring attitude of prayer to simply focus on hearing the Lord and sitting still at his feet. Set a timer for 20 or 30 minutes. I recommend engaging in this practice twice per day. Contemplative prayer will be developed even further in the chapter on meditation.

Pray: Abiding in the Vine

As I recovered from burnout, Sister Harriet, my spiritual director, gently turned me towards contemplative prayer. This opened a door for me to simply abide in the presence of my dear Lord. He revealed much to me through the passage in John 15:1-8 about abiding in the vine, and I have since shared those insights at many Pastors' Sabbath Retreats. While reading through this chapter on abiding in the vine, ask yourself if you hear Jesus calling you to come closer, sit in His presence more, and simply soak in His love for you.

The Importance of Abiding

How do you live the Christian life in a way that you finish well? How do you live a full working life with family in this world and survive personally without burning out, dropping out, or withering up and dying in your own soul? How do you stay spiritually healthy? In particular, when focusing on the care of others in the pastorate, how do you stay spiritually healthy? Survival and finishing well begins by clinging solely to our source of life, which is Christ himself, as Paul reminds us in Philippians 1:21: "For to me, to live is Christ, to die is gain."

But what does this mean practically? Christ intervenes in our lives if we give Him a chance, so part of the initiative comes from Him. But what is our part? How do we do it?

We must be constantly abiding in the vine. Abiding in the vine involves clinging to him, staying in His presence, calling ourselves to consciousness of His Presence, taking orders from Him, and being alert to His voice. Let's take a moment to read Jesus' words found in John 15 on this subject.

> *I am the true vine, and my Father is the gardener. He cuts off every branch in me that bears no fruit, while every branch that does bear fruit he prunes so that it will be even more fruitful. You are already clean because of the word I have spoken to you. Remain in me, as I also remain in you. No branch can bear fruit by itself; it must remain in the vine. Neither can you bear fruit unless you remain in me.*
>
> *I am the vine; you are the branches. If you remain in me and I in you, you will bear much fruit; apart from me you can do nothing. If you do not remain in me, you are like a branch that is thrown away and withers; such branches are picked up, thrown into the fire and burned. If you remain in me and my words remain in you, ask whatever you wish, and it will be done for you. This is to my Father's glory, that you bear much fruit, showing yourselves to be my disciples.*
>
> *~ John 15:1-8*

If we stray from Him and do not bear fruit, according to the first half of verse two, He will cut our branch off the vine. This is a form of discipline, setting us aside on a shelf or out of the way until we have corrected this situation in our life. In a vineyard, if a branch on a grapevine does not bear fruit, it usually grows very large and lies on the ground in the dirt. Its leaves become filthy. However, when we come to him, He will cleanse us, tie up our branch so that it can bear fruit again, forgiving us of our sin.

This second half of verse two tells us that when we do bear fruit He prunes us. I remember being pruned in Mittersill, Austria in 1998. My husband and I were working as missionaries in a castle, which operated as a 150-bed Christian retreat center. I did counseling in the castle, taught counseling in the study center in the castle, and was beginning to teach counseling in the surrounding countries of Eastern Europe and Russia. My ministry was bearing fruit. Suddenly, we lost our job at the castle where we spoke English and moved to Innsbruck, Austria. I was suddenly back to square one, and I became very depressed. I had to learn Austrian German (I knew high German, having learned the language in Germany), and I had to discover what my ministry would be in a new place. I was starting over. I went to a church service in Switzerland and an elder in the church who did not know me prayed over me. He saw a vision of me standing in a field looking very forlorn because the Lord had taken my sickle away and I could not harvest the field. He told me to look up to see the Lord driving up in a combine and inviting me to climb up into it with Him. The Lord told me that from now on, I would not harvest just one field but many fields. I went on working with German-speaking churches in Switzerland, Austria, and Germany to counsel many and teach counseling in churches. I was amazed at the results of the Lord's pruning, because afterwards my ministry began to bear much more fruit than ever before.

However, when we bear much fruit, His Word tells us that He issues an invitation to deeper intimacy with Him in John 15:5, 7, and 8. We have the choice to remain in Christ and abide in Him and deliberately and consciously bask in His Presence. It is perhaps a choice to practice contemplative prayer where we spend time in solitude and silence just listening to the Lord. This is different than intercession where we are asking Him for things and constantly doing the talking. Instead, we sit in His Presence. We listen to Him. We receive His perspective on our lives. We cannot hear Him if we do not choose to listen for His gentle whisper. Elijah heard Him in a still small voice on the mountain in 1 Kings 19. Elijah was in solitude in the cave. He had just walked for 40 days through the desert to get to this mountain. It was then that he heard the Lord:

> The LORD said, "Go out and stand on the mountain in the presence of the LORD, for the LORD is about to pass by." Then a great and powerful wind tore the mountains apart and shattered the rocks before the LORD, but the LORD was not in the wind. After the wind there was an earthquake, but the LORD was not in the earthquake. After the earthquake came a fire, but the LORD was not in the fire. And after the fire came a gentle whisper. When Elijah heard

it, he pulled his cloak over his face and went out and stood at the mouth of the cave.

At Jesus invitation, we must choose to step into deeper intimacy with Him and practice this kind of contemplative prayer. We need to deliberately spend time alone with Him, stepping out of our busy lives of service.

In order to intentionally abide in the vine, I personally practice the prayer of silence, as some of my Catholic friends have called it. I light a candle to focus my attention. I set the timer on my iPhone to 20 minutes so that I do not have to be concerned about time. I sit quietly in God's presence and listen to him. I use a Christian mantra to help me focus my attention. Sometimes, this is the hardest thing for me to do because I think of everything else that I should get up and do at these moments. I have learned to keep a pen and paper beside me to write the thoughts down so I can release them to be attended to later. Then my mind can settle back down, and I can focus on the Lord again. A better way might be to simply ignore these thoughts. I need to let go of these things and stand naked before the Lord in the stillness. It seems that everything in the world will present itself to me to keep me from entering this time of solitude. I must choose to put aside the noise of my thoughts and listen to the Lord: He will speak in the stillness. Perhaps it is only a gentle whisper as He spoke to Elijah.

Maintaining Our Priorities in Ministry

Those of us who are called to ministry often forget that we are first called to a person: Jesus. But we are also called to people. We must learn the balance of these two that can only come in abiding in the vine. As we abide with Jesus, we also become envisioned, equipped, and empowered to live out his commission.

Dallas Willard encourages us to also have right priorities in order to survive in church ministry. He lists three priorities every minister must have:

1. Be saturated in the presence of the Trinitarian God.
2. Make apprentices of Jesus.
3. Arrange for and go with His plan for inner transformation in the lives of these apprentices. Implement this plan as a natural outworking of His touch. As John Wimber used to say, we commit our lives to "doin' the stuff" that Jesus did.

This instruction is found in the Great Commission of Matthew 28:18-20:

> *Jesus came and told his disciples, I have been given complete authority in heaven and on earth. Therefore, go and make disciples of all nations, baptizing them in the name of the Father and the Son and the Holy Spirit. Teach these new disciples to obey all of the commands I have given you. And be sure of this: I am with you always, even to the end of the age.*

We personally need to abide in the vine in order to get our priorities straight as Jesus commanded. This is when we want to take a good hard look at Jesus, copy him, and place Him directly in the center of everything in our lives on all levels. This is how we run the race to which He has called us with perseverance. We are told in Hebrews:

> *So, my dear Christian friends, companions in following this call to the heights, take a good hard look at Jesus. He's the centerpiece of everything we believe, faithful in everything God gave him to do. Moses was also faithful, but Jesus gets far more honor. A builder is more valuable than a building any day. Every house has a builder, but the Builder behind them all is God. Moses did a good job in God's house, but it was all servant work, getting things ready for what was to come. Christ as Son is in charge of the house. Now, if we can only keep a firm grip on this bold confidence, we're the house!"*
>
> *~ Hebrews 3:16, The Message translation*

> *And let us run with endurance the race that God has set before us. We do this by keeping our eyes on Jesus, on whom our faith depends from start to finish.*
>
> *~ Hebrews 12:1-2*

So after getting close to Jesus and keeping our eyes on Him, we must obey Him if we love Him. Obedience is tied to our love. In other words, we must do what He does. Out of love for Him, we will obey Him.

We also must submit to His commands, which are to love God and our neighbor as ourselves as John instructs:

> *Dear friends, let us continue to love one another, for love comes from God. Anyone who loves is born of God and knows God. But anyone who does not love does not know God – for God is love . . . And God himself has commanded that we must love not only Him but our Christian brothers and sisters too.*
>
> *~ 1 John 4:7,8,21*

If we do the above, there will be an order to our ministry: communion, community, commission. The priorities are communion with the Trinity, community with our brothers and sisters, and commission to the world. Most of us want to go from communion straight to commission. This is out of order. We must copy the Trinity who begin in community with each other as they minister to us.

The Role of Community

Abiding in the vine (Jesus) also involves abiding with His body, the church. Most of us have our theology on this correct and our hearts agree, but we do not know how to do this practically. I have read two books lately on this topic, which have helped me tremendously. They are Scott Peck's book *The Different Drum* and Larry Crabb's book *The Safest Place on Earth*. I personally have made a decision that I will try to bring community on earth wherever I am planted. My experience has taught me that community involves creating a safe place where people can be themselves and risk being vulnerable. This is a place where love dwells, acceptance abounds, and souls are affirmed and cared for.

After I read Peck's book, I realized that I had done what he teaches in three recovery groups for women who had been sexually abused, which I had co-led in a Minirth Meier New Life Clinic in Langley, B.C. I did not know exactly why so much healing had taken place in these three groups, and then the light bulb went on. It had been an emotionally safe place for these people to grow and heal, a place where an atmosphere of love existed. Confessing our sins to one another, being vulnerable, showing our weaknesses in relationships builds bridges to one another; sharing strengths builds walls. The disease of modern man, according to Henri Nouwen in his book *The Wounded Healer*, is loneliness. Building community begins to heal this disease of loneliness. To build an emotionally safe community, we must put relationships above work and ministry. Working out of an emotionally safe community will foster a better environment for long-term survival in church ministry. Unfortunately, many of our churches do not have strong community and are very unsafe places. But we can work to obey our Lord and bring an atmosphere of love into them by being leaders who obey Jesus' commands and wish to survive for the long haul all the way to the finish line.

Finishing a life of ministry well is not simple. There are many choices we make in the process of a lifetime that factor into our spiritual health. We need to bask in the presence of the Trinity and remain there, connected to light and life, in order to survive in church ministry. We must receive the pruning from our Lord as His way of making us more fruitful in His service. We need to step towards Him into deeper intimacy as well, basking in the love of His Holy Presence. We should seek to align our priorities to the Great Commission. Then we need to have the order of ministry in line—communion, community, and commission—not leaving out community in the middle, which gives us our support in ministry. Communion with the Trinity, abiding in the vine, is what mainly sustains our life. If we get disconnected, we will surely wither and die like the grapes. It manifests as burnout or falling away before finishing our job well at the finish line. Let us abide in the vine.

Going Deeper

After reading the above chapter, thoughtfully answer these questions, which may apply to your situation. Write a journal entry with "Abiding in the Vine" as your focus and express what and how you could change this next year to single-mindedly focus your life on your relationship with Christ.

Passage: John 15: 1-8

How does one accomplish a major life task and at the same time survive personally without burning out, dropping out, withering up, or dying spiritually?

Where has the Lord disciplined you and/or pruned your lifestyle during this last year? How have you walked out that correction in your life?

Is basking in His presence a central part of your lifestyle? How have you done this during this last month? How does your schedule reflect this?

Do you see single-mindedness in your life? How can you aim your life at what he aims His at without wavering during this next year? How would your schedule reflect this? What needs to change?

Where do you see surrender in your life? Has obedience been an easy journey for you during this past year? Where do you need more surrender or obedience in your life?

Is the order of your life prioritized appropriately? What action do you need to take to rearrange it and to bring it into the correct order of communion, community and commission?

Pray: Intimacy with God

We touched on the topic of intimacy with God during the discussion on abiding in the vine, but the subject deserves a more in depth exploration. Before we can know how to have intimacy with God, we need to know what intimacy is.

Webster's New World Dictionary says that *intimacy* comes from the Latin word *intimus,* which means *within.* The first meaning is "inmost; most inward; essential," as in the intimate structure of the atom. The second meaning is "most private or personal," as in one's intimate feelings. The third meaning is "closely acquainted or associated; very familiar," as in an intimate friend.

A friend of mine who does personal growth seminars talks about intimacy as allowing someone to "in to me see." Another person needs to be close to me to be able to see into me. Creating intimacy in a relationship is allowing another person to come close and see within. It involves openness, honesty, and vulnerability. A goal in the Christian journey should be to walk in intimacy with God.

Four Kinds of Intimacy

The Baker Encyclopedia of Psychology on page 603 tells us that there are many kinds of intimacy. The article speaks of four types in particular:

1. **Spatial** intimacy or physical nearness, as in being close by, like two inmates in a prison cell.
2. **Psychological** intimacy, like two friends who share their feelings with each other, who know and share each other's psychological functioning.
3. **Sociological** intimacy is when people's fortunes are linked together in social functioning, like members of a family, marriage partners, or members of a tribe. What befalls one has direct bearing upon others in the relationship.
4. **Sexual** intimacy, as with marriage partners or those in a sexual relationship.

The encyclopedia goes on to say:

In tribal societies (as with the bulk of Old Testament societies) there would have been little reason to distinguish between spatial and sociological intimacy. Those related to each other shared both types, and usually one's psychological intimates were also from one's family, either immediate or extended. In many such societies, there is no concept of friend. In contemporary societies one typically chooses where and with whom one will share sociological intimacy. Generally persons are even more careful about where and with whom they establish psychological and sexual intimacy.

Our space age travel has allowed the separation of types here. As the meaning of marriage has changed from dutifully obeying one's family or tribe in your marriage choice to that of a free choice of mate in Western society, the kinds of intimacy idealized as occurring within marriage have increased. There is little hint of psychological intimacy between husbands and wives in the Old Testament and similarly little, if any, in the times of the New Testament. But modern marriage is idealized as providing a structure for all four kinds of intimacy; the "perfect marriage" features spouses who live together (spatial intimacy), personally enjoying each other's company, sharing with each other financially, and choosing to share sexual intimacy with each other and no one else. Reality is that these are rarely the facts of life. Intimacy in the Western society is on the decline in families, marriages, and friendships, according to recent studies.

Description of Intimacy with God

As a Christian, we are called to have a personal relationship with God. The Bible has many images of our relationship with God such as the shepherd with his sheep, a father with his child, or a lover with his beloved. This relationship suggests very close communion as John 14:23 suggests that Jesus and His Father would come to his disciples and make their home with them to create union with the Trinity.

Jesus Called Us Friends

Mentioned above in John 15:1-17 where Jesus speaks of the metaphor of his disciples being like a branch and His being like the vine, He tells us to "abide in Him." Verses 13-15 are very important in indicating just how intimate Jesus views our relationship with Him. He calls us His friends. Listen once again to this portion below from the New Living Translation.

> I am the true vine, and my Father is the gardener. He cuts off every branch that doesn't produce fruit, and he prunes the branches that do bear fruit so they will produce even more. You have already been pruned for greater fruitfulness by the message I have given you. Remain in me, and I will remain in you. For a branch cannot produce fruit if it is severed from the vine, and you cannot be fruitful apart from me.

> Yes, I am the vine; you are the branches. Those who remain in me, and I in them, will produce much fruit. For apart from me you can do nothing. Anyone who parts from me is thrown away like a useless branch and withers. Such branches are gathered into a pile to be burned. But if you stay joined to me and my words remain in you, you may ask any request you like, and it will be granted! My true disciples produce much fruit. This brings great glory to my Father.

> I have loved you even as the Father has loved me. Remain in my love. When you obey me, you remain in my love, just as I obey my Father and remain in his love. I have told you this so that you will be filled with my joy. Yes, your joy will overflow! I command you to love each other in the same way that I love you. And here is how to measure it—the greatest love is shown when

*people lay down their lives for their friends. You
are my friends if you obey me. I no longer call
you servants, because a master doesn't confide
in his servants.* **Now you are my friends,** *since
I have told you everything the Father told me.
You didn't choose me. I chose you. I appointed
you to go and produce fruit that will last, so
that the Father will give you whatever you ask
for, using my name. I command you to love
each other.*

This portion speaks of a breathtaking intimacy, so
close that the Father and Son actually come and dwell
within our physical body and are one with our soul and
spirit. I think that this would include all the four types of
intimacy mentioned above plus some because of being
joined together spiritually. Notice that Jesus' description
speaks of our knowing everything that He has heard from
His Father. It also speaks of our loving Him, which can be
interpreted to mean our obeying His commands. When we
are deeply in love with another person, it is a privilege to
fulfill their every wish, much less their commands.

I think that it is better said that we *may* obey Jesus'
commands. Reflect on the metaphor a moment of the branch
and the vine. The branch literally draws its very life from
the vine, getting life-giving water and nutrients coming
through to it. We need to draw deeply on Jesus'
supernatural life in order to live the life of the kingdom
down here on earth. We cannot afford to be separated from
Him or it will mean our spiritual death. Intimacy with Him is
life-giving in this sense.

Now let us look at some examples of others who have found this intimacy with God to see if we can glean a little bit about how to get there. Maybe we can catch a glimpse of the way through the example of their lives.

Quotes from Saints and Examples

"Life is a call to be. It is a call to forget separated self, and to become totally lost in our God. Our focus must shift from what we get out of life to offering ourselves as a gift to our Lover." This is a quote from Bill Volkman, who was the founder and editor of *Union Life* magazine. He invites us to observe Mary and Martha in Luke 10: 38-42.

Jesus Visits Martha and Mary

As Jesus and the disciples continued on their way to Jerusalem, they came to a village where a woman named Martha welcomed them into her home. Her sister, Mary, sat at the Lord's feet, listening to what he taught. But Martha was worrying over the big dinner she was preparing. She came to Jesus and said, "Lord, doesn't it seem unfair to you that my sister just sits here while I do all the work? Tell her to come and help me."

But the Lord said to her, "My dear Martha, you are so upset over all these details! There is really only one thing worth being concerned about. Mary has discovered it—and I won't take it away from her."

Why wasn't Mary paying any attention to what Martha was doing? It was because she was totally lost in the presence of her beloved Lord. Mary wasn't thinking about what she could do for Jesus, or what He could do for her. She was completely absorbed in her love for Him and in His unconditional love of her. Mary's behavior might seem radical, but she was right. We need to stop spending all our time learning "about" God and "working for" Him. We need to spend some time practicing His presence and just adoring Him. There is a healthy balance of Mary and Martha's positions to be had.

Practicing the Presence

Brother Lawrence says in his book *Practicing the Presence of God* that this "is the concentration of the soul's attention on God, remembering that He is always present." He calls it by several names like a loving look at God—a remembrance of Him, attention to God, silent communion with God, confidence in God, or the life and the peace of the soul. It is, perhaps, the fixing our eyes on Jesus of which Hebrews chapter 12 speaks.

Contemplative Prayer

Bill Volkman's single practical suggestion on how to live the Christian life is "to experience the prayer of silence—the wordless prayer. Practice contemplative prayer. Don't just read, talk about and analyze it. Faithfully practice basking in God's presence in solitude and silence twice a day for ten minutes for thirty days. If you do this—with loving God and being attentive to His presence as your primary goal—you will be a practicing contemplative for the rest of your life."

I think this is a very interesting suggestion, which would prove well for you to try. In fact, I challenge you to try it! I have been doing it for 20 minutes each morning and evening and have found that it brings peace, joy, and stability into my life. This practice is like a daily anti-anxiety pill for me. I use a single word mantra to help me focus.

Inward Life

What Jeanne Guyon says about intimacy with God is very insightful:

> *Your way to God begins on the day of your conversion, for conversion marks your soul's initial return to God. From that moment you begin to live and have your being by the means of His grace. After your conversion, your own spirit—the human spirit (which is deep within your inmost being)—is touched by God and is made alive and functioning.*

> *Your spirit, in turn, invites your soul to compose itself and to turn within, there to find the God who has newly come to reside at the center of your being. Your spirit instructs your soul that, since God is more present deep within you, He cannot be found anywhere else. Henceforth, He must be sought within. And He must be enjoyed there, alone.*

> *Therefore, from the very beginning, you find great joy in knowing that your Lord is within you and that you can find Him and enjoy Him in*

*your inmost being. From the very beginning of
your conversion or from the very outset of your
life in Christ, it is possible for you to know that
what you are to pursue is that inward life."*

That inward life is another way of saying intimacy
with God. And, if I understand Madame Guyon correctly, the
place to do this is deep within one's inner being. Jesus told
us that his Kingdom is within us.

Learn to Be—Come Home to Rest

Thomas Keating in his book on contemplative prayer,
Open Mind, Open Heart, says to his readers:

*Learn to rest in faith in Him, learn to just "be"
unto God. For a few minutes, perhaps twice a
day, stop all the words and analyses, and just
"come home" to the inner center of your being,
where your human spirit is one with the
indwelling Spirit of Christ.*

The question is, "Are we able to be still enough to
become intimate with the One who dwells within?" Can we
quiet ourselves to find our center and come to rest with God
and experience the peace of His Presence?

Be Still or Get Quiet Inside

Psalm 131 is talking about this coming into silence
and solitude with God:

*A song for the ascent to Jerusalem. A psalm of
David.*

*LORD, my heart is not proud;
my eyes are not haughty.*

123

> *I don't concern myself with matters too great*
> *or awesome for me.*
>
> *But I have stilled and quieted myself,*
> *just as a small child is quiet with its mother.*
> *Yes, like a small child is my soul within me.*
>
> *O Israel, put your hope in the LORD—*
> *now and always.*

So, this coming to rest or finding the peace of his presence as Keating talks about requires humility and the openness, honesty, and trusting attitude of an infant as it nurses at it mother's breast.

Get into Heart instead of Head—Be instead of Do or Think

Another way of thinking about intimacy with God is to think about just being with him, or hanging out together. Being is hard. We find it hard *to be* with our human spouse or with a friend. We even find it hard *to be* with ourselves sometimes. We compulsively have to have something *to do or think about.* But God longs for us to just come and be with Him. That is what He made us for—not to chase everywhere looking for Him or another spiritual experience or for holiness. He made us to enjoy him. And this is almost impossible for us to do to enjoy him with our heart instead of trying to figure Him out with our head or serve Him with our body by doing. This kind of hanging out with God requires our living out of the space of our heart and not out of our head.

It is the most important thing in our life, and yet it is hard for us to believe that God really wants an intimate relationship with us. We think, "I need to get my act together before I can have a relationship with Him." But we are made to share everything with him—every moment, every hope, every dream, and every fear. This is the purpose of our creation!

Knocking to Bring Light into Every Room in the House

There is a famous painting by Holman Hunt hanging in St. Paul's Cathedral in London called *The Light of the World.* It depicts Jesus with a lamp in his left hand, knocking on a vine-covered plank door. The Bible verse found in Revelation 3:20 is engraved in the picture's massive, gold-etched frame and it reads:

"Behold I stand at the door and knock
If any man hear my voice and open the door
I will come into him and will sup with him
And he with me."

Bill Volkman in his book *Basking in His Presence* relates how this verse addresses nonbelievers but also how it is a continuing invitation to believers throughout their entire lives to allow Christ further and further or deeper and deeper into our heart home, allowing him into every room of the house to completely fill us with His light and push all the darkness out of our souls. We don't want a hidden dark closet where Christ is not allowed to enter.

C.S. Lewis speaks of the New Creation in *The Last Battle* as "further in and farther up" which brings the same picture to mind as the suggestion about this painting.

Lamb of God with His Bride

Another way to imagine this intimacy is to look at the image of Jesus as the Lamb of God with his bride, the church. In Revelations 19:7, the metaphor of the bride of the Lamb is spoken of with these words: "Hallelujah! For the Lord our God, the Almighty, reigns. Let us be glad and rejoice and honor him. For the time has come for the wedding feast of the Lamb, and his bride has prepared herself. She is permitted to wear the finest white linen." (Fine linen represents the good deeds done by the people of God.)

William McNamara talks about what this breathtaking intimacy with God might be like. He says,

> *It is God (who is love, and love is diffusive, meaning that this love goes in every direction without being able to be controlled) who takes the initiative, unites Himself to us, keeps us alive by His creative and attentive presence, and with no violence, but with the gentle fury of an irrepressible and invincible love, touches us where we are most free and invites us, seductively, into the intimate and infinite love—life of the Trinity.*

What we need to do is sensitively recognize who we are—brides of the Bridegroom—and be aware of what is going on: we are being led to the bridal chamber. So our relationship with Christ is like an initial marriage union! Wow! It takes my breath away to imagine myself as the bride of the Lamb who is being led to the bridal chamber to unite with Him!

Song of Songs—Love is Stronger than Death, Unquenchable

This description immediately reminds me of the imagery in the Songs of Songs 8:6-7 passage where it says:

> *Place me like a seal over your heart, or like a seal on your arm. For love is as strong as death, and its jealousy is as enduring as the grave. Love flashes like fire, the brightest kind of flame. Many waters cannot quench love; neither can rivers drown it. If a man tried to buy love with everything he owned, his offer would be utterly despised." This is the kind of love that our Lover, Jesus Christ has for His bride, you and me. Wow! Isn't this amazing? Doesn't it just blow your mind? So contemplative prayer or silent prayer invites us to just come and sit at Jesus' feet like Mary did and bask in his loving presence and be consumed by this fire of priceless love that cannot be quenched or drowned.*

Let me tell you a personal story. It was the fall of 1983 and I had just graduated from New College Berkeley in CA with a Master's Degree in Christian Studies, and we had moved to Vancouver, BC, with our three children, aged thirteen, ten, and three, where my husband, Peter, had taken a job teaching New Testament at Regent College. My mini-thesis had been written on women in ministry with the title "The Theory and Practice of Lay Ministry by Women in the Plymouth Brethren." I had come to a conclusion in my paper that women were equal to men in the kingdom of God as Paul talks about in Galatians 3:28. So, I said to Peter that we needed to renegotiate the way we ordered our marriage because we had too much of a patriarchal pattern in it. He said that he could not focus on anything new but on the new preparations for his courses in Regent College that he had to teach. Sorry! Wow, did this ever disillusion me! I was all stimulated and fired up from having studied and having grown intellectually and from having been inspired by the writing of my thesis!

Peter had typed the thesis on his new Kapro computer, which he had bought that year, so he knew full well what this was all about, and he agreed with me theologically. However, I learned that theory and practice are two different things. At any rate, he could not focus on our marriage, but needed his energy for lecturing. Mind you, I am not faulting him here and have long since forgiven him for the hurt that it caused me; so do not get worried about our marriage. It is doing better today than it ever has. However, at that time, this unmet expectation of changing our marriage pattern to be more equal was not met, and I became very depressed. At this particular time, I was taking a course from

Dr. James Houston who was then principal of Regent College in Vancouver. I went in to get some help to write the paper in that course and ended up signing up for spiritual direction with him.

Later I shared with him in one of our sessions that our marriage was in a rough spot and I was depressed. Then I told him the above story about my thesis and Peter's not being willing to renegotiate with me. Dr. Houston sympathized with Peter, saying that he was in a very hard place at the moment adjusting to teaching at Regent, adjusting to Canada, and adjusting to our church. (We were both in the leadership of a Plymouth Brethren church in the Vancouver area.) Actually, we both had a lot on our plates. He told me to turn away from Peter towards Jesus. He told me to take my demands off Peter in our relationship. He also gave me an assignment that day: I was to read the entire book Song of Songs until I could see Jesus Christ as my Bridegroom. He told me to read it several times a day if I could. (By the way, I might comment that I thought that this was a weird idea, and it felt very strange to me when I began.) However, my marriage wasn't working too well at the moment, I was tired and lonely after getting my Master's and moving to Canada, and I was willing to try anything. So, I began that evening and read the 8-chapter book all the way through. I read it twice a day for about five weeks, seeing nothing different and still thinking that the idea was rather weird. The other part of my assignment was to journal about my experience with reading this book and chronicle any changes in my relationship with Jesus or others.

As my sixth week of reading began, something changed. It was as if Jesus had walked into my room and sat down with me as I read. I somehow sensed His presence with me. Do not ask me to explain this: all I can say is that my room was pregnant with peace, warmth, and light, and I knew that He was there. Then at the end of the week, I dared in my mind's eye to look over at Him, and He was staring at me with love in His eyes. I began to cry as I realized how deeply He loved me–more than any person on this earth. His love broke my pride. That morning at the end of the sixth week, I wrote in my journal that I could at last begin to see that Jesus, the Lover of my soul, loved me with an intense, intimate love. My response was tears: I was emotionally overwhelmed, not quite being able to comprehend what it meant, but I sensed that it is true. Jesus indeed is my Bridegroom, and His love is stronger than death. The fire of this love cannot be quenched with the water of many rivers, and it cannot be bought for any price.

This experience had a strange effect on my marriage: it improved! From the strength, which came from Jesus' love for me, I was empowered to forgive Peter and to see him in a new light. I could appreciate the extreme pressure he was under, having driven a U-Haul truck from Sewickley, PA, to Vancouver, having unloaded it, having begun a new job at Regent College, having adjusted to a new country, and having begun to lead in a new church at the same time. I began to pray for Peter that some of the love of His

Bridegroom, Jesus, would enable him to carry out all his responsibilities including those of being a husband.

That year our relationship greatly improved; but we never reworked the structure of our marriage. I had lost my desperation and my expectation that he would change, and I could lift that expectation off him. My depression also lifted, and my anger dissolved in forgiveness. I have a tender spot in my heart about the gorgeous poetry in the Song of Songs. Here is an ironic tidbit: Peter and I began our honeymoon by reading the Song of Songs together. I dare say that the book has taken on a far deeper meaning to me since that day on August 19th in 1967 when Peter and I were newly married. Intimacy with God had a very positive effect on my most important relationship, my marriage.

So as we have looked at some examples from church history, gleaned knowledge from saints old and new, examined Scripture, and listened to what it has to say about intimacy with God, we will now look at this topic with a human perspective (if we can be down to earth here) at some advantages and disadvantages of our intimacy with God.

Advantages of Intimacy with God

Life

We have seen that this intimacy is necessary to stay alive and to grow, recalling the metaphor of the vine and the branches: intimacy with God is a life-nurturing sustenance!

Purpose of Our Creation

Another positive reason to pursue this intimacy is that it is the reason we were created: to enjoy our relationship with God and so God could enjoy His relationship with us. He created us to give back to Him a gift that no one else in the world can give Him. Do you know what that gift is? It is our love! He greatly desires our love. It is wonderful to get lost in His love as Mary did when she sat at Jesus' feet. Jesus told Martha that this is the better part. But Jesus desperately wants our love back and allows us the freedom of choice. Our creation purpose of intimacy with God brings joy, as we love him back.

Rest to the Soul, or Peace

Another reason for this intimacy is that it brings rest to the soul and peace. It is a coming home and finding the Father waiting for us with His open arms of unconditional love like the Prodigal Son did in Luke 15. The compassionate Father heart of God, which constantly has our best at heart and forgives us of our sin, is too good to believe. But it brings true peace to the soul as we come home and rest.

Healing and Wholeness

Another great advantage of this pursuit of intimacy with God is that as we connect with our compassionate heavenly Father, our soul is healed of its deepest wounds. Our Father becomes our personal psychotherapist who knows us very well because He created us. We are restored to our original, intended power of gifted creativity, the way He envisioned us at our creation. Flora Slosson Wuellner gives us a glimpse of how God's healing power works in our soul:

> Our fear, when healed becomes intuitive, empathic compassion and sensitivity towards others. Our destructive anger, when healed, becomes a passion, a hunger and thirst for justice and righteousness. Our perfectionism, our compulsion to organize and dominate, when healed, becomes released, joyous power to build and create. Our inertia and withdrawals, when healed, become increasing powers for peace and integrity. Our possessiveness, our jealousies, and our physical addictions, when healed, become growing released powers to become lovers and healers to the world around us.

This is a beautiful picture, which brings hope. Henri Nouwen talks about us as the wounded healers, like Jesus.

Contentment

Thomas Keating tells us of another advantage of our union with God. It is contentment!

> Lacking the experience of divine union, we feel alienated from ourselves, God, other people and the cosmos. Hence, we seek substitutes for the happiness for which we are predestined but which we do not know how to find. This misguided search for happiness is the human predicament that the Gospel addresses. Happiness can only be found in the experience

> *of union with God, the experience that also*
> *unites us to everyone else in the human family*
> *and to all reality. This return to unity is the*
> *good news that Jesus proclaimed.*

And, this union brings with it real contentment.

Disadvantages

God is good and His intentions towards us are good, so absolutely everything about this pursuit of intimacy with Him is good for the human being from God's perspective. However, it may not always look that way to us. It may falsely seem to be bad or hard or the worse of the two paths, thus my calling these aspects disadvantages.

Costs Our Life and We Lose Control

From our perspective, the first disadvantage is that this pursuit will cost our very life and all that we have. The costs are huge! A second disadvantage, if viewed from a human perspective is that this pursuit will cost us the control of our lives. God takes over and we become His slave if we pursue intimacy with Him from our perspective.

Go through Darkness

After we make a decision to pursue intimacy with God, especially at the beginning of our walk with God, it is easy to sense His presence, and we go from one time of glorious basking in His presence to another. Then as we mature a bit, it may seem that the Lord withdraws from us. In the book *The Dark Night of the Soul* by St. John of the

Cross, the believer is said to enter at a certain point in our walk with the Lord the dark night of the soul where we cannot clearly sense the presence of God. It feels as if He has abandoned us. Because we cannot sense that He is there, we sometimes assume that He is not there. There is a real difference between the Lord's presence being there and our sensing that the Lord's presence is there. We will look at some of these illusions later when we mention some blocks to intimacy with God.

Desert

There is another image that comes to mind as I think about disadvantages, and that is the image of the desert. As Jesus began His public ministry, the Spirit led him into the wilderness or the desert. This was a time when earthly comforts were stripped away, and Jesus was tested as He fasted for 40 days. In the preface of a book called *Formed by the Desert,* written by Joyce Huggett, Dr. James Houston writes the following:

> *Desert spirituality is central to the lives of authentic men and women. There are many reasons for this. Primarily, man can derive his existence from the earth, and seek only earthly ways of living. Or he can recognize he does not live by bread alone, so then he looks to God and his Word, by which to live. Made in the image and likeness of God he then seeks to live detached from the false allurements of the flesh.*

Dr. Houston goes on to say that Joyce Huggett challenges us to reflect whether we derive our meaning and existence from God or from the earth alone. Certainly from a human perspective not enlightened by the light of Christ, man would seek to find his own way. God's way can sometimes feel like a desert experience similar to the dark night of the soul as mentioned above.

Pain

Another disadvantage of the pursuit of intimacy with God is the pain that comes with the pruning that a vine must undergo to produce fruit as we looked at above in the John 15 passage. Pain of all sorts—emotional, mental, physical and spiritual—comes with growth, which needs to be pruned back to enable the branch to produce more fruit. Another metaphor speaks of this pain as the refining fire of God, and this fire feels very hot at some points in our life.

Sometimes, this pain comes as shattered dreams, which all of us experience during life. Here are some of the painful experiences I have endured:

1. I did not see my Dad until 13 months old. He was in the South Pacific with the US Marines during WWII. I was scared to death of him and would not allow him to hold me when we first met. It took him until I was two years old to befriend me.
2. Shortly after beginning school, I contracted polio and landed in the hospital and had to do all my homework at home for the first three months until I had learned to walk again.

3. On the way to university in August, my family was in a three-car accident and I did not begin university until January because my leg was broken, my pelvis was cracked, and I had a crushed vertebra in the base of my spine. All the members of my family were seriously hurt except my sister.

4. My third child, a daughter, died at six weeks of crib death, and I had a miscarriage six months after her funeral. Then I had our son one year later and had to leave him at age 16 in Canada as we became missionaries in Austria. (This last child, our son, had brought healing and joy into my life when he was born; and it was he whom I had to lay on the altar and tell the Lord that I loved Him more than my son.)

5. I began a counseling ministry in three places: in the Brethren Church which Peter and I co-pastored for five years, in Regina, Saskatchewan, and in Schloss Mittersill in Austria. I had to leave all three, and each leave-taking represented a shattered dream in some sense for me. The ministry in the Brethren Church collapsed in about a year or two of our leaving, due to a church split. The Caring Place in Regina came into being about two or three years after I left. My name is on a plaque in the front hall as one of the founders, but I was not there for it's opening and

never got to counsel there and have never visited it. A counseling ministry was beginning to build at Schloss Mittersill, and we were asked to leave. One of the reasons was that the administration did not want to build a counseling ministry because they had other agendas like the Conference and Retreat Center and the Study Center. They still sent people to me for counseling in Innsbruck after I left, but our leave-taking was a shattering of a dream for me.

Every one of these shattered dreams in my life has been a time of extreme pain and extreme growth for me. During the time of the funeral of our daughter, I experienced the presence of God in a tangible way. The grieving process for her and for the miscarriage that followed is one of the lowest valleys of my life, but I may have grown the most walking through that dark valley of the shadow of death. The Good Shepherd never left me, although it was hard to see him through my tears.

Leaving my son in Canada represented excruciating pain for me! Even though he was in favor of our going and told us that he thought it was the Lord calling us to Europe, I had nightmares that it would be harmful for him if we were to leave him. Guess what—all the nightmares came true. Just before we left, his girlfriend of one year broke up with him, breaking his heart. He cried himself to sleep the first three weeks we were gone because he was so lonely. He was shocked that he missed us. He wrote us every day with email for six months. One week after school began for him in September, with our neighbor girl in the front seat of the car, he totaled our Honda Wagovan that we had left for him to drive. Three weeks later, his new bicycle, which was now his transportation, was stolen at school. Then he lost his weekend job of stacking chairs at church because he got into an argument with our pastor. At Christmas, he was in a basketball accident and had to have surgery on his jaw and eat baby food for the next 6 weeks. When I saw him again the next summer, I was bemoaning how horrible the year had been for him, and I told him how sorry I was that we had left him all alone. Then he told me not to worry because he had grown more during that past year than he had grown in the 15 years that had preceded it. His pain had caused a huge growth spurt.

Growth Is Very Painful

This story is a peek into the shattered dreams in my life where most of my spiritual growth has taken place. I could have given you a lot of Biblical examples like Naomi and the losing of her husband, two sons, and one daughter-in-law, and yet she became the great, great, great, etc. grandmother of Jesus Christ. Or Paul, with his 3 shipwrecks, imprisonments, beatings, being stoned, and yet he may have been the greatest missionary in history. The Apostle Peter, so tradition has it, was crucified upside down and yet was the rock on which Jesus built his church. Then church history gives us numerous other examples with persecution of the saints like Joan of Arc who was guided by heavenly voices and won a great victory for France against England but was burned at the stake as a heretic. Or John Wycliffe who translated the Bible into common English but who was later declared a heretic and whose books, it was later degreed, should all be burned and his body exhumed.

Assuming that the glory and joy of knowing Jesus so outweighs everything else imaginable, as it does in my life, in the Apostles Peter's and Paul's lives, and all the other saints' lives that we've mentioned, how can we not decide to pursue intimacy with God? So having made our decision, we must ask the following questions: How do we become intimate with God? What steps do we take?

How to become Intimate with God

There is no simple answer here! There is no "1, 2, 3; you are free" formula to finding intimacy with God. This is a long journey that begins with a decision and we will spend the rest of our lives walking out. On the other hand, one could argue that it is very simple: to be single-mindedly focused on loving Jesus Christ with all our heart, soul, mind and strength. When Jesus was asked what was the most important commandment, He replied,

> *Hear, O Israel! The Lord our God is the one and only Lord. And you must love the Lord, your God with all your heart, all your soul, your entire mind, and all your strength. The second is equally important: "Love your neighbor as yourself."*

These verses are found in Mark 12: 29, 30. The journey is simple but not easy.

However, there are some steps, which we can take which might point us in this direction. Some of these steps have been already mentioned above but bear repeating.

Steps towards Becoming Intimate with God

Bruce Wilkinson reminded us of a key when he said that we must make a decision to place intimacy with God as the top priority of our lives. Then we might ask, 'What does that mean?' 'What does it look like?' or 'How do I do that?'

In Deuteronomy 30 and in Romans 10, God spells it out rather simply: "Choose life in order that you may live. . . by loving the Lord your God, by obeying his voice, and by holding fast to him." In effect, God is saying, "Just focus on your love relationship with me and you will have found the meaning of life. Then you can live life to the fullest." This simple command was given to the children of Israel after their 40 years of wandering in the wilderness. The time had come to enter the Promised Land and to enjoy the inheritance that God had planned for them.

But before God gave Israel this simple formula of "Love God and you will live," God first laid down the Law in detail in the first 29 chapters of Deuteronomy. The people were ready to throw up their hands and shout, "That's impossible!" We cannot keep all those hundreds of laws. This is exactly what God wanted them to understand and feel. He would have said, "You're right!" So, God met them at their point of need and promised them in Deuteronomy 30:6 that he will give them the wherewithal for a love relationship with Him – a changed heart. "The Lord your God will circumcise your heart . . . to love the Lord your God."

God also promises us the gift of a changed heart so that we too, by faith, can choose to love Him and live. "For this commandment, (to love) which I give you this day is not too difficult for you, nor is it out of reach . . . The word is very near you, in your mouth and in your heart, that you may observe it."

The answer is very simple and very close to us here on earth. We don't have to go up to the heavens or cross the sea to get what we need. The kingdom and the power is already within us. God told the Israelites in the wilderness, and He tells each of us the same thing through Paul today. "The word is very near you, in your mouth and in your heart."

Let's remember as we begin talking about steps to pursuing intimacy with God that we do not want to make a new law, because we will not be able to keep it. We want to make a plan that will assist us in our journey towards loving God.

We need to figure out what fits us and what will help us take some steps in our pursuit. We could begin by copying someone else's plan like Bruce Wilkinson's, which I mentioned above. I also mentioned Bill Volkman's single practical suggestion for living the Christian life, and that was to experience the prayer of silence—the wordless prayer. Another name for this kind of prayer is contemplative prayer or centering prayer, as we have talked about above. But, somebody might ask, "Well, how on earth do I do that?"

On page 47 of his book, *Basking in His Presence*, Bill Volkman quotes M. Basil Pennington, a Cistercian monk who gives us his method in the following steps:

> *Sit relaxed and quiet.*
>
> *Be in faith and love with God who dwells in the center of your being.*
>
> *Take up a love word and let it be gently present, supporting your being with God in faith-filled love.*
>
> *Whenever you become aware of anything else, simply gently return to the Lord with the use of your prayer word or mantra.*
>
> *Close by letting the "Our Father" (or some other familiar prayer) pray itself through you.*

All we have to do is "be still" and consent to His presence within. We focus our minds on nothing but His presence. As we do this in faith twice a day, for twenty or thirty minutes each time, we will be engaging in the prayer of silence, as taught by the Desert Fathers and others for centuries. It seems simple, but you might be amazed at how difficult it is.

I suggest you start by trying contemplative prayer for five minutes. Move your chair so that you can get comfortable, sit back, and relax. Use some word from

Scripture that will aid you in thinking of God like: Abba, Father, home, Jesus, peace, rest, yes, or joy. Say this word gently to yourself only when your mind wanders. The goal is to hold our Beloved close and not to evaluate our time; just "to be" or to bask in His loving Presence.

There are many other tools I have learned and tried through the years. To give you some ideas as an example, here is a list of the disciplines that I have placed in my life that help in my personal pursuit of intimacy with God. Be adventurous and begin trying some of these exercises.

- First discipline of my day: make my very first thought, "Jesus"!
- Read Scripture each day: OT passage, a Psalm, and NT passage; sometimes reading a small book in the Bible over and over to saturate myself in it. I need to begin with Scripture, the plum line for truth.
- Keep a spiritual journal—I often write out prayers, write about my feelings, reread to get perspective on my life, and remind myself of answered prayers.
- Practice contemplative prayer for 20 or 30 minutes each morning and evening.
- Make plans in a Daybook, writing out appointments for the week. Set these spiritual disciplines in my schedule.
- Do aerobic exercise for 30 minutes daily and care for my body.

- Read a portion of a spiritual classic every day.
- Say Evening Prayer from the Anglican Prayer Book with my husband, Peter after supper each evening, thanking God together for our day and cuddle for a few minutes, while drinking a cup of tea.
- Do some serious Bible study or research once or twice per month.
- Worship in church each Sunday, attend a small group weekly prayer meeting, and worship privately once per week at least by singing, dancing, playing piano before the Lord, or singing along with a CD.
- Tithe, and also give generously to special projects and people that God brings to my attention.
- Fast on Fridays during Lent, and fast periodically during the year. Whenever Peter is gone, use the time alone for solitude and silence and sometimes for fasting.
- Make a yearly one-week retreat to fast and pray, thus putting solitude and silence into my yearly schedule.
- Take food for a food pantry to church once per month.

These are some of the spiritual disciplines in my life. I mention them not to say, "Look at me," but to offer some concrete examples of how one person has done this. Your list will look very much like you, just as my list looks like Judy. My list changes periodically depending on my present needs. It represents where I'm weak or broken and need help.

Blocks to Intimacy with God

Just as we must be proactive in engaging in activities to promote intimacy with God, so also we much also actively ward against the things that block our intimacy with Him. Here are some warnings about things that might hold you back.

You might miss God because you think you know all about how things need to be, know about who He is, know about how he will act, or whatever the false knowing may be. This is the terrible thing about religion. While Jesus was on the earth, the religious people "knew"—so they got rid of Jesus. The highest knowledge of God is to know God as unknowable. We can never put him in a box. We can never figure him out completely. We can never predict exactly how he will act. He will always surprise us! He is the unfathomable One. He is the Sovereign Almighty One— infinitely creative.

Our false image of God might block us from intimacy with Him, especially if we see Him as the distant one who does not care about our lives. We might see Him as the stern one who will condemn us and punish us. We might see him as a Sugar Daddy or Santa Claus figure that is there to just give us candy and everything nice whenever we ask. Then when our earthly Dad dies young of cancer, even though everyone was praying for his healing, we can no longer find God. Our view of God needs to be corrected by reality, to find the God of the Bible, the one true God. We need to not only find what Scripture says about God but we must also believe what it says and trust God as our good Father. We need to correct the false image of God modeled to us by our parents from whom we were taught who God is as we experienced their authority in our lives.

Shattered dreams, as Larry Crabb puts it in his book by that name, may keep us from finding intimacy with God. The pain is so great from this shattering that we just cannot find God anymore. Because of our pain we might be Christians with a Buddhist belief system. Buddha believed the following things:

- Life is suffering.
- The cause of all suffering is desire. (People suffer because they desire what they do not experience.)
- The way to end suffering is to end desire.
- Spend your life learning to eliminate desire. Follow the eight-fold path of Buddha, which shows you how.

Jesus directs us to a different path than Buddha as Larry Crabb suggests:

- Jesus tells us that life includes suffering but life is good. He has made a way for us to satisfy our deepest desire in the midst of unrelieved pain.

- The cause of all suffering is separation. We are separated from God—and from our own deepest desire, our longing for God—and we're therefore deceived into looking elsewhere for joy. That sets us off on the ultimate wild goose chase and that is the basis for our addictions. Nothing but God satisfies our most profound desire.

- The way to handle suffering is to discover your desire for God. Then everything both good and bad becomes redemptive. It moves us toward the God we desire. Enter your thirst. Face your disappointment. Eventually, you will seek God for these four things:
  - Forgiveness for your failure to love.
  - The love you desire.
  - Empowerment to love others.
  - Hope that one day you will revel in love freely given and freely received in a perfect community of lovers.

The new life provided through Jesus must be accepted as a gift of love. We then spend the rest of our days discovering our desire to know God better, and we come to realize that it's a desire whose satisfaction no shattered dream can thwart.

God's restraint is another thing that might disillusion us and make us want to give up on our search for intimacy for God. His restraint is often to make us so thirsty for Him that nothing could then hold us back from Him again. We might feel abandoned by Him at these times.

Feeling good is not the goal. Making 'God look good' to any who watch us live our lives is the goal.

Going through darkness is always part of this path. It is then that God is probably doing His deepest work in us. Think of Jesus' three hours of darkness on the cross when redemption was being won for us: He yells at God, "My God, my God, why have you forsaken me?"

Hope for Joy

We could go on and on, but I will end on this note: Our journey to joy takes us through shattered dreams, as Larry Crabb puts it. But there is hope: a new way to live is available to us, a way that leads to a joy-filled encounter with Christ, to a life-arousing community with others, and to a powerful transformation of our interior worlds that makes us more like Jesus. Our journey will end in joy! As we come nearer to God and learn to be able to stay near, we will experience a deep, peaceful joy, which comes from this intimacy that will saturate our entire being and our entire life. Of course our eternal end is to be with Him forever so our joy will never end! Hallelujah!

The Apostle Paul encourages us onward in Philippians 3:

Whatever happens, dear brothers and sisters may the Lord give you joy. I never get tired of telling you this. I am doing this for your own good.

Watch out for those dogs, those wicked men and their evil deeds, those mutilators who say you must be circumcised to be saved. For we who worship God in the Spirit are the only ones who are truly circumcised. We put no confidence in human effort. Instead, we boast about what Christ Jesus has done for us.

Yet I could have confidence in myself if anyone could. If others have reason for confidence in their own efforts, I have even more! For I was circumcised when I was eight days old, having been born into a pureblooded Jewish family that is a branch of the tribe of Benjamin. So I am a real Jew if there ever was one! What's more, I was a member of the Pharisees, who demand the strictest obedience to the Jewish law. And zealous? Yes, in fact, I harshly persecuted the church. And I obeyed the Jewish law so carefully that I was never accused of any fault.

I once thought all these things were so very important, but now I consider them worthless because of what Christ has done. Yes, everything else is worthless when compared with the priceless gain of knowing Christ Jesus my Lord. I have discarded everything else, counting it all as garbage, so that I may have Christ and become one with him. I no longer count on my own goodness or my ability to obey God's law, but I trust Christ to save me.

*For God's way of making us right with himself
depends on faith. As a result, I can really know
Christ and experience the mighty power that
raised him from the dead. I can learn what it
means to suffer with him, sharing in his death,
so that, somehow, I can experience the
resurrection from the dead!*

*I don't mean to say that I have already
achieved these things or that I have already
reached perfection! But I keep working toward
that day when I will finally be all that Christ
Jesus saved me for and wants me to be. No, dear
brothers and sisters, I am still not all I should
be, but I am focusing all my energies on this one
thing: Forgetting the past and looking forward
to what lies ahead, I strain to reach the end of
the race and receive the prize for which God,
through Christ Jesus, is calling us up to heaven.*

*I hope all of you who are mature Christians will
agree on these things. If you disagree on some
point, I believe God will make it plain to you.
But we must be sure to obey the truth we have
learned already.*

*Dear brothers and sisters, pattern your lives
after mine, and learn from those who follow
our example. For I have told you often before,
and I say it again with tears in my eyes, that
there are many whose conduct shows they are
really enemies of the cross of Christ. Their
future is eternal destruction. Their god is their
appetite, they brag about shameful things, and
all they think about is this life here on earth.
But we are citizens of heaven, where the Lord
Jesus Christ lives. And we are eagerly waiting*

for him to return as our Savior. He will take these weak mortal bodies of ours and change them into glorious bodies like his own, using the same mighty power that he will use to conquer everything, everywhere.

Dear brothers and sisters, I love you and long to see you, for you are my joy and the reward for my work. So please stay true to the Lord, my dear friends.

Prayer Tools: The Examen

During my journey of learning more about spiritual disciplines, I have discovered many wonderful tools to facilitate prayer. I've found that the *Consciousness Examen*, a spiritual discipline made popular by St. Ignatius of Loyola, goes a long way to cultivate the attitude of gratitude in my life. This discipline, often simply called the Examen, is the daily habit of stopping to reflect on the best thing and the worst thing about each day and then recording it in a spiritual journal or sharing it with a friend or intimate. Then by looking for recurring themes, one can cultivate an attitude of gratitude in one's life and get direction therefrom.

Introduction to the Examen

The Examen is a prayer model for discerning the activity of God in our lives and a way to respond to his loving presence. It is part of a wider body of work by Saint Ignatius (1491-1556) called *The Spiritual Exercises.* These exercises were originally written by Ignatius for retreat directors. The Examen as it is practiced today is a contemporary adaptation of one of Ignatius' execises.

God is speaking to us by ways in which many of us are unaware. Paying attention is a learned skill. We must learn to pay attention to God, to our souls, to our physical bodies, and to others. The Examen is a way to learn how to pay attention to God's activity in our lives and hear what he has to say to us about what we have recently experienced. The Examen is a kind of debriefing that allows you to process your day with God. The Jesuit Priest Dennis Hamm talks about the Examen as a "rummaging backwards through the 'drawer of your day' (or of your stuff) to find the God moments."

The Examen has been explained as having five parts:

1. Become aware or conscious of God's presence—a prayer of enlightenment

2. Review your day with gratitude—prayer of reflective thankfulness

3. Practical survey of actions—honestly listening to discern your interior consciousness and your emotions, becoming aware of the Spirit's movement in your soul

4. Contrition and sorrow—a natural outflow of our heart in faith, noticing our weaknesses and shortcomings, but relishing in the joy of having a Savior who forgives.

5. Hopeful resolution for the future—looking toward tomorrow with God's light.

The Apostle Paul held the strong conviction that God is active in the lives of those who love him, and God is working in all the events of our lives, towards forming our inner lives into the likeness of Christ. Romans 8:28-29 tells us, "We know that in all things God works for the good of those who love him, who have been called according to his purpose. For those God foreknew he also predestined to be conformed to the likeness of his Son, that he might be the firstborn among many brothers." While this is an often-quoted verse, many people miss God's activity in their lives by simply being unaware of the ways in which God is working for their good and conforming us into the likeness of his Son. The Examen is a way to discern God's activity in both the positive and negative forces that come our way.

The Examen helps one become conscious of movements in the soul. By asking these two simple questions, *what gave me life today* and *what was life-draining*, you can begin to see similar patterns, especially when a record is kept over a period of 30 days. This spiritual discipline helps discern life direction and purpose. St. Ignatius calls these indicators in our lives *consolations* and *desolations*. Consolations give us a deep sense of connection in our lives to God, others, and ourselves. Desolations give us the loss of this sense of connection with the presence of God, others, or ourselves. Taking the time to reflect on our days helps us discover what things give us life. This exercise guides us in identifying and doing more of those things that give us life and leave out those things that are life draining. Ignatius believed that God speaks to us through our consolations and desolations, so understanding them is vital to our walk with Him.

Some of the characteristics of consolations are that they can be encouraging, strengthening, joyful, satisfying, or they give inner freedom that opens you up or gives you a sense of vitality. They are life affirming. Some of the characteristics of desolations are that they leave you feeling discouraged, sad, full of anxiety, trapped, or they close you down or cause you to feel overburdened. They are life draining. The following illustrations depict the dynamics of consolations and desolations in our lives.

The two movements of the soul are depicted
here. The top spiral shows desolations, which
spiral down into self, closing you down.
The bottom spiral describes
consolations, which spiral outward away
from self.

157

How might we IMAGE these opposing spiritual movements that happen in our inner life?

Consolation	Desolation
Directs our focus outside and beyond ourselves. Lifts our hearts so that we can see the joys and sorrows of other people. Bonds us more closely to our human community. Generates new inspiration and ideas. Restores balance and refreshes our inner vision. Shows us where God is active in our lives and where he is leading us. Releases new energy in us.	Turns us in on ourselves. Drives us down the spiral ever deeper into our own negative feelings. Cuts us off from community. Makes us want to give up on the things that used to be important to us. Takes over our whole consciousness and crowds out our distant vision. Covers up all our landmarks. Drains us of energy.
Expands your heart until it is big enough to contain other people and their needs, and makes it light enough to fly to God.	Shrivels and shrinks your heart and makes it so heavy that it sinks to the lowest point of your experience.
DRAWN	DRIVEN

A misconception of the Examen may be that the perusal of our consolations and desolations is a merely inward-looking exercise. The opposite is true. It's an exercise in walking with God through the unexplored territories of your own life. The focus is on His activity. In the Examen, you ask God two things. First, you seek His help to review your day and show you what energized you and what disempowered you. Second, you ask Him to give you His perspective on your consolations and desolations. This interaction can lead to real wisdom and guidance for your life and deepened fellowship with God.

There are many scriptures that highlight the importance of the self-awareness and God-awareness that the Examen facilitates. These are just a few:

> *Search me, O God, and know my heart; test me and know my anxious thoughts. See if there is any offensive way in me, and lead me in the way everlasting.*
>
> *~ Psalm 139: 23-24*

> *And this is my prayer: that your love may abound more and more in knowledge and depth of insight, so that you may be able to discern what is best and may be pure and blameless until the day of Christ, filled with the fruit of righteousness that comes through Jesus Christ—to the glory and praise of God.*
>
> *~ Philippians 1:9-10*

> *Finally, brothers, whatever is true, whatever is noble, whatever is right, whatever is pure,*

159

whatever is lovely, whatever is admirable – if anything is excellent or praiseworthy – think about such things.

~ Philippians 4:8

What Others Say about the Examen

The Prayer of Examen produces within us the priceless grace of self-knowledge.

It has two basic aspects, like the two sides of a door. The first is an examen of consciousness through which we discover how God has been present to us throughout the day and how we have responded to his loving presence. The second aspect is an examen of conscience in which we uncover those areas that need cleansing, purifying, and healing.

~ Richard Foster

As you do the Examen, you are listening to both God and yourself, since God speaks within your deepest experience.

The Examen makes us aware of the moments that at first we might easily pass by as insignificant, moments that ultimately can give direction for our lives ... Insignificant moments when looked at each day become significant because they form a pattern that often points the way to how God wants to give us more life.

~ Dennis, Sheila, and Matthew Linn

We cannot attain the presence of God. We're already totally in the presence of God. What is absent is awareness. This is the core of the

spriritual journey—learning to discern the
presence of God, to see what really is . . . Most of
us learn to discern God's presence by first
looking for it in the rearview mirror. That is the
value of a prayerful review of the day.

~ *Richard Rohr and David Benner*

The Examen for Beginners

There are many ways to practice the Examen. I have
found the following simplified model to be a great starting
place. Before you begin, find a place where you can relax
and be quiet. Take a few moments to get settled.
Acknowledge to God His love for you and His involvement in
your life.

Step One: Consolations

Ask God to bring to your awareness the moment
today for which you are most grateful. Ask Him to show you
how and where He gave you strength, where you felt the
most energized, the happiest, and the most alive. Sometimes
it helps if you go back in your mind to the moment you woke
up and then fast-forward through your day (like you would
fast forward through a DVD) and ask Him to show you your
consolation. If more than one consolation comes to mind,
choose one to focus on.

After you locate the moment or event, step back into
it and let yourself relive the joy of that moment. God Himself
practiced this type of reflection at the end of each day of
creation. After working all day, He reminded Himself that "it

161

was good." Thank God for the consolation you experienced. Allow yourself a few moments to enjoy your consolation again by stepping back into the life-giving emotions you experienced.

Then ask God to show you what about that event gave you life. What was said and/or done that made that moment so life-giving? Sit still and wait for Him to respond. If you journal, you might want to write out your dialogue with God. If He does not say anything at this time, simply rest in His love for you.

Step Two: Desolations

Ask God to bring to your awareness the moment today for which you are least grateful, where you experienced sadness, shame, failure, anger, or where you felt life and energy being drained from you.

After you locate that moment or event, step back into it and relive the feelings without trying to change or fix it in any way. Let yourself revisit your pain. It is important that you are honest with your painful emotions. Many of us have been taught to diminish or make light of our pain. This does not benefit us in the long run; it is much more important to be honest with yourself and with God. When I am journaling this exercise, I simply write out what I am feeling, such as "this makes me so angry, and I feel really humiliated."

Ask God what about the desolation made you so angry, sad, helpless, or shameful. Listen to what He has to say. Again, if you journal, you might want to write down your insights and conversation with God. Ask God to comfort you and fill you with his love and sit in silence for a few moments.

Step three: Thankfulness

This third step is critical to your experience of the Examen. After meditating on your desolations, take time to give thanks for whatever you have experienced during the day. Thank God for being present with you in your consolations and desolations. This daily practice of gratitude will foster a lifestyle of thankfulness despite your circumstances or experiences and will help you be aware of God's presence as you experience moments of consolation and desolation in the future.

The Ignatian website www.ignatianspirituality.com describes Ignatian prayer as follows:

Ignatian prayer is imaginative, reflective, and personal. St. Ignatius Loyola encouraged people to develop an intimate relationship with a God who loves them and desires the best for them. Ignatius Loyola trusted human desires. He believed that our deepest desire is to return God's love. Ignatius Loyola also trusted feelings. He believed that feelings of joy and sorrow, peace and distress, were important indicators of the path toward fruitful decisions and deeper union with God. At the heart of Ignatian prayer are the Spiritual Exercises and the Daily Examen.

Models of the Examen

Over the five hundred year history of the Examen, Jesuits and others have developed many versions of the Examen. They are like successive editions of a great textbook. They are based on the same insight and ideas, but they differ in order to emphasize certain things and to adapt to diverse audiences. Below are some elucidations of this spiritual discipline by some of those who have been shaped by it.

The Particular and Daily Conscience Examen by Ignatius

Perhaps it would be best to start with St. Ignatius himself. In the original version of the Examen, Ignatius had the goal of improving the practitioner's life by looking for your sins and seeking to throw them out. Thus he advised that you begin the exercise when you arise by praying to guard yourself with diligence against sin. After the noon meal, you should practice the first Examen, and then after the evening meal, you should practice the second Examen. He instructed his monks to compare the number of times they failed in the first half of the day with the number in the second half of the day and compare the number of sins from one day to another and also from one week to another. The goal was to become better at identifying sinful habits, throw out all sins, and live a holy life.

Ignatius talks about there being three voices inside of us: our own human voice, one from the good Spirit, and one from the bad spirit. He wants us to be able to discern between these three. Therefore, he instructed his monks to learn discernment by practicing this version of the Conscience Examen:

1. Give thanks to God our Lord for the benefits received.
2. Ask grace to know our sins and cast them out.
3. Ask account of our souls from the hour that we rose up to the present Examen, hour by hour, or period by period: and first as to thoughts, and then as to words, and then as to acts.
4. Ask pardon of God our Lord for the faults.
5. Purpose amendment of our lives with His grace. Then finish with the Our Father.

George Aschenbrenner, SJ, wrote a definitive article in 1972 that enlarges the scope of the Examen from this first Ignatian version and says that it must be seen in relationship to the discernment of spirits. It is a daily, intensive exercise of discernment in a person's life. We moderns who value spontaneity in our lives disagree with the Greek philosopher Socrates who claimed that "the unexamined life is not worth living." But there are two spontaneous voices inside, a good one and a bad one; we must discern between the two. Doing the Examen is a means of learning which is what voice inside of us. When the Examen is related to discernment, it becomes the Examen of Consciousness rather than of Conscience. The Examen of Conscience has narrow moralistic overtones, and its prime concern is with the good and bad actions we have done each day. The Examen of Consciousness, using discernment, speaks of how God is affecting us and moving us. The Holy Spirit must be invited into our heart to discern this movement of God. Ignatius deliberately put the Examen at the beginning of his Spiritual Exercises because it is an indispensable tool to detect God's presence and discern His will through close attention to the subtle interior movements of God's spirit. It is the cornerstone of Ignatian prayer.

The Examen is a time of intense prayer, which requires regular, reverent, and quiet contemplation— completely upstream from how our culture asks us to live in constant noise, distraction, and motion. We are actually developing a heart with a discerning vision when we regularly practice the Examen. We learn to live God's love in our daily situation. It becomes an exercise that so focuses and renews our specific faith identity that we should never omit it, as St. Ignatius warned his monks. When busy during the Council of Trent, he was asked by his fellow Jesuits what prayers could be left out and Ignatius answered anything but the Examen. He said that "finding God in all things" is what life is all about, and this is the core goal of the Examen. At first it is stylized and feels very formal for the beginner, but for the mature saint at the end of his life, it becomes like breathing, this determining what is God in our daily movement and living.

The Consciousness Examen by Peter Filice, SJ

A modern day Jesuit named Peter Filice has interpreted St. Ignatius' Examen in the following way:

The Examen is a gift to find God in all things. It is a way to discover God in our own heart. By it we grow sensitive to our own spirit and discern God's Spirit.

Filice modified Ignatius' five steps in his version of the Consciousness Examen.

1. Recall that you are in God's presence.

   "For in Him we live and move and have our being. As some of your own poets have said, 'We are His offspring'" (Acts 17:28).

   I am a creature in the midst of creation. Look at all with love.

2. Review my day with gratitude.

   In the words of Mary: "My soul glorifies the Lord for the   Mighty One has done great things for me—holy is His Name." (Luke 1: 46, 49)

   Recall the events of my day. Take stock of the gains. Look at the gifts with which I had to face the day. Pause in thanksgiving!

3. Ask for the Holy Spirit's help.

   "When the Spirit of truth comes, he will guide you into all the truth. He will not speak on his own; he will speak only what he hears, and he will tell you what is yet to come"   (John 16:13).

Look at my own heart with honesty and patience without condemnation.

4. Review how I am living today.

"Love does not dishonor others, it is not self-seeking, it is not easily angered, it keeps no record of wrongs"(1 Corinthians 13:5).

Review events of my day and explore the context of my actions. What and who were in my day? What were my hopes and hesitations? Was my heart divided? Do I see an opportunity to grow? Then pray that the Lord give you habits of freedom: loving and honoring others with patience, peace, and contentment.

5. Look with hope toward tomorrow.

"'Can I not do with you, house of Israel, as this potter does?' declares the Lord. 'Like clay in the hand of the potter, so are you in my hand, house of Israel'"(Jeremiah 18:6).

Look on myself with compassion. Express sorrow for my sin and ask for forgiveness. Give the Lord thanks for His grace.

End with the Lord's Prayer.

Notice that this version of the Examen is very similar to St. Ignatius' original, but is put into our language and is slightly modified.

Questions of Consciousness Examen by Linns

In their book *Sleeping with Bread*, Dennis Linn and Sheila Fabricant Linn with Matthew Linn say:

For many years, we have ended each day the same way. We light a candle, become aware of God's loving presence, and take about five minutes of quiet while we each ask ourselves two questions.

They go on to describe paired questions, which help them identify the consolations and desolations of the day:

For what moment today am I most grateful?
For what moment today am I least grateful?

When did I give and receive the most love today?
When did I give and receive the least love today?

When did I feel most alive today?
When did I most feel life draining out of me?

When today did I have the greatest sense of belonging to myself, others, God, and the universe?
When did I have the least sense of belonging?

When was I happiest today?
When was I saddest?

What was today's high point?
What was today's low point?

Then we share these two moments with each other and give thanks to God.

169

Matt says he does the Examen because of his pessimistic outlook to remind him of what went right in his life. Dennis says that he is an optimist and needs it to help him appreciate the moments for which he is not grateful that God speaks through. Sheila says that the Examen helps her to be who she is and not who she thinks she ought to be. As a child, she was not encouraged to trust herself and she learned to be ashamed of her needs and desires. The Examen has helped her trust herself.

The Linns expand the Examen by explaining that it can be shared in a small group, in a family, or done alone by journaling for 30 days and noticing patterns over the month. There are no rules: you can share the positive question only; you can do it for a day, week, year, or a lifetime. You can vary it by asking what you are grateful for in another person and letting them know. It is about reflection on your life, choosing the best, and leaving out the worst.

The Examen as Presented by Hamm

Dennis Hamm, SJ, who teaches theology at Creighton University in Omaha, Nebraska, presents the five steps of the Examen slightly differently in easier-to grasp wording.

1. Pray for light. We need the Holy Spirit's graced understanding.
2. Review the day in thanksgiving. Fondle your beautiful gifts, which came during the last 24 hours—gifts of existence, work, relationship, food, and challenges.

3. Review the feelings that surface in the replay of the day. (Hamm explains that our feelings, positive or negative, painful or pleasing, are the clear signals of where the action was during the day.)

4. Choose one of those feelings and pray from it. Choose the remembered feeling that most caught your attention. The feeling is a sign that something important is going on. Spontaneously express the prayer that surfaces as you attend to the source of the feeling, such as praise, petition, contrition, cry for help, or healing.

5. Look toward tomorrow. Using your appointment calendar if that helps, face your immediate future. What feelings surface as you look at your tasks? Turn this into prayer—whatever it is.
   End with the Lord's Prayer

Hamm talks about nine benefits coming from praying the Examen:

1. One always has something to pray about because we never run out of the last 24 hours.

2. Developing the attitude of gratitude is worth every minute in this spiritual discipline.

3. Facing the Lord honestly right where we are in our mess being very present to God is a huge plus instead of trying to come to God in our Sunday best.

4. Using this prayer also helps us learn to respect our feelings. Feelings count, even though morally neutral until we decide how we will act upon them.

5. By praying from our feelings, we can gain freedom from them, not having to be dominated or manipulated by them.

6. This prayer helps us discover what we need to bring to confession. We become aware of our shortcomings as we stop and examine our actions, thoughts and feelings.

7. Inner healing can happen by praying through our emotions.

8. We learn that God is intimately involved with us in our lives. He's not a sort of clock-maker God who wound us up, set our lives in motion, and then abandoned us. No, He is involved daily in our lives, ever present with us.

9. We leave our "do it yourself" lives and respond daily to God's love and grace in our lives. When we hear His voice, we answer and obey.

Hamm is not saying that by remembering or by paying attention to our felt experiences, we are listening to God. Instead, he is saying that it is the interface between God and his creatures where God's voice is heard; it is in relationship with Him that we learn to recognize His voice and His loving acts and respond accordingly.

Reflection and Our Active Lives by Fleming

David L. Fleming, SJ, expounds on the Examen in his book *What is Ignatian Spirituality?* The goal of the spiritual life, as Ignatius conceived it, is to "choose what better leads to God's deepening life in me." This is a dynamic goal. We are to *choose* to freely unite ourselves with God. Most of the time this means that we are to join with God in active work in the world. Fleming explores this Ignatius' exercise from yet another angle: reflection.

According to Fleming, our active lives rest on a foundation of reflection. Ignatian spirituality teaches us to discern the footprints of God in our own experience. It shows us how to look back on our lives and sift through our memories in order to see the way God has been dealing with us over the years. It teaches us how to find God in the present moment—in the relationships, challenges, frustrations, and feelings that we are experiencing today. The tools and methods of Ignatian spirituality instill in us habits of prayerful, thoughtful reflection.

Because the word Examen seems to indicate a kind of introspection, probably the greatest emphasis should be placed on the Examen as praying. Ignatius tries to emphasize this point by making his first point of the Examen one about gratitude to God.

Fleming's version of the Examen, taken from his book *What is Ignatian Spirituality?* is as follows:

A Prayer to God

God, thank you.
I thank you, God, for always being with me, but especially I am grateful that you are with me right now.

God, send your Holy Spirit upon me.
God, let the Holy Spirit enlighten my mind and warm my heart that I may know where and how we have been together this day.

God, let me look at my day.
God, where have I felt your presence, seen your face, heard your word this day?
God, where have I ignored you, run from you, perhaps even rejected you this day?

God, let me be grateful and ask forgiveness.
God, I thank you for the times this day we have been together and worked together.
God, I am sorry for the ways that I have offended you by what I have done or what I did not do.

God, stay close.
God, I ask that you draw me ever closer to you this day and tomorrow.
God, you are the God of my life—thank you.

Sometimes our prayer can get formal and abstract. The Daily Examen keeps our feet on the ground. This reflective, Spirit-led review of the day grounds our prayer in concrete reality. Because we are God's sons and daughters living in a world that he loves and sustains, we can be assured that we can hear his voice in our lives in this world.

There is one final advantage to making a habit of the Daily Examen: We will never run out of things to pray about. Sometimes prayer gets dry. Sometimes we wonder what to say to God. The Examen eliminates these problems. As long as we have twenty-four hours to look back on, we will have hundreds of things to talk to God about—and to thank him for.

~ *David L. Fleming, SJ,* What Is Ignatian Spirituality?

Creative Applications of the Examen

One way to hear God better is by living reflectively and practicing the Examen to develop discernment. There are many ways to incorporate it into our daily lives. Here are some of the ways that I have found helpful. You can be creative, after learning from each of the Jesuits, and create your own as I have done here.

1. *Choose a small group* of two of three friends or your spouse and do the Examen at the end of the day or once per week. You could choose to write in your journal and then share with each other. It may be helpful to use the Linns' format of desolations and consolations and choose one of the paired questions to discuss.

2. *At a dinner party* as people have their dessert, go around the table telling each other the best part of your day or week or the best time since you last met together. We've done it in our family with our children and grandchildren at Sunday

175

noon dinner, using only the positive question. The youngest might be guided to say "our good dinner" if they cannot think of anything else. We have done it in our Foyer Group, using both questions. At a birthday party, I've asked the birthday child what the best and worst part of their year has been.

3. *Write a birthday card or letter* and insert everything good that you can think of about that person or everything that they have kindly done for you and thank them for it, affirming them and encouraging them. I've done this for two of my sisters-in-law this past year and included one in this chapter.

4. *Journal for 30 days and look for themes* in your journal to provide guidance for life. Ask yourself what things give you life and what things are life draining.

5. *Do an Ecological Examen*, discerning your relationship to the Creator and His creation. I have also included an example of an ecological Examen in this chapter.

6. *Look at your marriage relationship* or a close friendship and ask what are the best things about this relationship and what are the worst things? Do more of the things that give you life and leave off the things that are life draining.

7. *Choose one of the methods of doing the Examen* and do it everyday in your journal. Focus on listening for the voice of God in your life. Choose the version of the Examen that grabs you or speaks to your heart most directly or the one you simply like the best. After a month has passed, go back and look for patterns, and journal about them. Or if you dare, create your own version and use it.

Sample Journal Examen

I spent the last ten days journaling my Examen to provide an example for you of how you can use the journal entries to see the movements of God in your life. This is what I learned about myself from the journal Examen:

1. I counted a point for my greatest consolation each of the ten days. There were five points for the best part of my day being service, three points for being in nature, and two points for getting intellectual stimulation.

2. I saw two places where I was disobedient to the Lord, and I had to ask His forgiveness. This made me sad. I realized that having to drive Peter for the last six months is teaching me to be dependent on the Lord; but I also saw resentment, so I had to ask the Lord to forgive me because I know that this is His doing. I need to learn contentment, so prayed for more contentment in my tomorrows.

3. I can see that meditating twice per day is having a calming affect on my life. Prayer is good for me!

4. I noticed that the worst part of my day had to do with getting angry three different times. Three other times, the worst part of my day had to do with getting my feelings hurt in a relationship. This helped me realize that I still need to work on my anger.

5. Two times, the worst part of my day was being disappointed because my expectations were not met. My perfectionistic expectations get me in trouble. My tomorrows must drop my expectations to bring peace.

Sample Birthday Letter Examen

On my sister-in-law Harriet's birthday, I sent her a personalized letter with an Examen prayer for her, which I've included here. Harriet wrote me back that she was having a particularly sad day and the letter had lifted her spirits. The prayer was just what she needed to hear.

Dear Harriet,

Today is your birthday! I want to wish you a very happy birthday by telling you how much I appreciate you. You have been an inspiration to me all through this long journey of Jim's getting cancer and dying, Suzanne's getting cancer and healing, Steve's becoming ill and not discovering why, and your own diagnosis of breast cancer and receiving therapy. Your faith in our Faithful God has never wavered and that has amazed me. You are an amazingly strong woman of faith. I admire you.

You are a beautiful woman who shines with the light of Christ daily. I've always been amazed at how gorgeous you are inside and out. Your talents such as singing, administrative skills, and writing are also so admirable. You are someone to whom I would point a granddaughter and tell her to copy you.

Even in your dark valley of grief as you have missed Jim, and then have begun to establish a new identity as a single woman, you are seen as an example to many. You have struggled long and hard and are coming out as gold, shining for God's glory.

I encourage you to keep on keeping on as you have done from the beginning. You have fought a good fight and have done well. I'm sure that the Lord is smiling at you today on your birthday and is saying, "Well done, my good and faithful servant!" He is singing over you with delight!

Here is a prayer to God based on the Consciousness Examen as inspired by Ignatius of Loyola and revised by David L. Fleming, SJ, which I'm using at a Quiet Day on April 6th. I thought that you might be inspired to pray this at the end of your birthday to examine what kind of day you had. This prayer exercise can be done in a daily journal to help you understand yourself and where God's presence is in your life— to help one live a reflective life and gain from lessons learned.

God thank you.
I thank you, God, for always being with me, but

especially I am grateful that you are with me right now.

God, send your Holy Spirit upon me.
God let the Holy Spirit enlighten my mind and warm my heart that I may know where and how we have been together this day.

God, let me look at my day.
God, where have I felt your presence, seen your face, heard your word this day?
God where have I ignored you, run from you, perhaps even rejected you this day?

God let me be grateful and ask forgiveness.
God I thank you for the times this day we have been together and worked together.

God, I am sorry for the ways that I have offended you by what I have done or what I did not do.

God, stay close.
God, I ask that you draw me every closer to you this day and tomorrow.
God, you are the God of my life – thank you.

Sample Ecological Examen

Joseph Carver, SJ, developed an Ecological Examen that challenges us to hear God's voice in and through His creation and out interaction with it. These are the questions Carver delineates to help us engage in an Ecological Examen in his article "Encountering a New World of Ignatian Contemplation" found on www.americanmagazine.org/issue/ecological-examen:

All creation reflects the beauty and blessing of God's image. Where was I most aware of this today?

Can I identify and pin-point how I made a conscious effort to care for God's creation during this day?

What challenges or joys do I experience as I recall my care for creation?

How can I repair breaks in my relationship with creation, in my unspoken sense of superiority?

As I imagine tomorrow, I ask for the grace to see the Incarnate Christ in the dynamic interconnections of all Creation.

Conclude with the prayer of Jesus: "The glory that you have given me I have given them, so that they may be one, as we are one, I in them and you in me, that they may become completely one, so that the world may know that you have sent me and have loved them even as you have loved me."

Prayer Tools: Lectio Divina

Lectio divina (pronounced lek-see-o de-vee-na) is an ancient prayer form that, for the first thousand years of church history, was an integral part of the Christian experience. It is a devotional way of reading, meditating on, and praying the Scriptures in a manner that enables the Word of God to penetrate deeply into our hearts. *Lectio divina* is built on the conviction that the Holy Spirit inspired the Bible and that the Holy Spirit continues to speak to us through the Scriptures. Through *lectio divina*, we can facilitate the word of God richly dwelling in us (Colossians 3:16). On a personal note, *lectio divina* has helped me to become obedient to God's words. His life-giving essence soaks into my very being, illuminating my way. As Thomas Keating said, "Prayer is not designed to change God but to change us." *Lectio divina* is one method of prayer that has proven to be very transformative.

Devotional reading of Scripture finds its roots in the Hebrew tradition. The early church adapted this practice and built on it. This practice began to be known as *lectio divina*, which is Latin for "divine reading." Saint Benedict, who created the basic foundational rule of the monastic movement in the West, placed prayer, work, and *lectio divina* as the three primary elements that gave rhythm to the daily life of Benedictine monks. Because of their dedication to the Scriptures and the other holy books of early Christianity, Benedictine monasteries were responsible for safeguarding much of the great literature during the Dark Ages. The Benedictines are also responsible for keeping alive the practice of *lectio divina* for the last 1,500 years.

Lectio divina was further refined by Guigo II, a monk who lived in France during the twelfth century. In his book *Scala Claustralium* (*The Ladder of Monastics*), Guigo writes,

> *One day I was engaged in physical work with my hands and I began to think about the spiritual tasks we humans have. While I was thinking, four spiritual steps came to mind: reading (*lectio), mediation (*meditatio), prayer (*oratio), and contemplation (*contemplatio). This is the ladder of monastics by which they are lifted up from the earth into heaven. There are only a few distinct steps, but the distance covered is beyond measure and belief, since the lower part is fixed on the earth and its top passes through the clouds to lay bare the secrets of heaven.*

At one time, *lectio divina* was seen as four interchangeable parts, but after Guigo, the four parts began to be seen as four progressive steps: *lectio, meditatio, oratio* and *contemplatio*. For the purpose of training and making simple things even simpler, Charles Bello, an Oklahoma pastor friend, has renamed the stages as Read, Reflect, Respond, and Rest. Bello also added a preparatory stage at the beginning, Ready, and an incarnational stage at the end, Return. He also added journaling as part of the whole process. Journaling is central to integrating the Word of God into our lives, because it is a concrete way of processing things on paper or on a computer screen.

Scripture is full of admonitions about the value of the Word of God in the life of the believer:

> For the word of God is living and active. Sharper than any double-edged sword, it penetrates even to dividing soul and spirit, joints and marrow; it judges the thoughts and attitudes of the heart. Nothing in all creation is hidden from God's sight. Everything is uncovered and laid bare before the eyes of him to whom we must give account.
>
> ~ Hebrews 4:12-13

> Let the word of Christ dwell in you richly as you teach and admonish one another with all wisdom, and as you sing psalms, hymns and spiritual songs with gratitude in your hearts to God.
>
> ~ Colossians 3:16

Lectio divina has proven over the centuries to be a valuable tool for Christians to pray, commune with God, and be transformed by Him.

What Others Say about *Lectio Divina*

> Lectio divina *is a way of life that develops "according to the Scriptures." It is not just a skill that we exercise when we have a Bible open before us but a life congruent with the*

> *Word made flesh to which the Scriptures give witness.*
>
> ~ *Eugene Peterson*

> *Three activities dominate the life of a Benedictine Monk: prayer, work, and* lectio divina . . . lectio divina *is about one thing: developing an intimate relationship with God by praying the scriptures he gave us.*
>
> ~ *Tony Jones*

Lectio divina is the most traditional way of cultivating friendship with Christ. It is a way of listening to the text of scripture as if we were in conversation with Christ and he was suggesting the topics of conversation. The daily encounter with Christ and reflection on his word leads beyond mere acquaintanceship to an attitude of friendship, trust, and love. Conversation simplifies and gives way to communing.

~ *Thomas Keating*

How to Practice *Lectio Divina*

If you are looking for a passage to start with, Charles Bello would encourage you to begin with passages that are already your favorites and see what else God might want to say. The Psalms are a natural for *lectio divina*, as well as John's letters, and the Sermon on the Mount. Ask God to show you where to start. Charles has added time recommendations only as a guide. You are free to adjust the time to fit your schedule and your own personal rhythm.

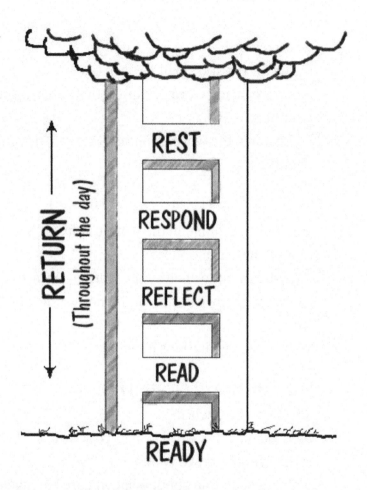

Step 1: Make yourself READY

Find a place where you can be quiet and undisturbed.
Choose a brief passage of scripture.
Ask God to meet you during this time of prayer.
You may want to journal *Lectio Divina*. This helps you
slow down and better process your thoughts, prayers
and reflections.

187

Step 2: READ / *lectio* (5 min.)

Read the passage slowly, letting your awareness rest on each word.

Listen for the still small voice of God.

Be aware of any word or phrase that catches your attention.

Write down the word or phrase that caught your attention.

Step 3: REFLECT / *meditatio* (10 min.)

Meditate and think on the word or phrase that caught your attention.

Use your mind to analyze the word or phrase.

Be aware of any emotion or memories the word may stir up.

Write your meditations down.

Step 4: RESPOND / *oratio* (10 min.)

Respond to the word.

Ask God why this word caught your attention. What is He trying to say to you?

Dialogue with God about what you are feeling or hearing. Write out your dialogue without editing it or worrying about spelling or grammar.

Take time to listen.

Step 5: REST / *contemplatio* (5 min.)

Simply rest in God's presence. Wordless, quiet rest in the presence of God is called "contemplation."

Short "breath prayers" are sometimes helpful when your mind wants to wander.

Say the word that caught your attention to bring your mind back also.

Step 6: RETURN (Many times during the day)

Keep returning to the passage and your reflections throughout the day / week.

Keep returning with the intention of prayerfully integrating the word into your daily life.

A Sample Outline of *Lectio Divina*

Below is a sample of short daily Scripture readings for *lectio divina* using Psalm 23.

Day 1
READ (5 min.): Psalm 23:1-3a—The LORD is my shepherd; I shall not be in want. He makes me lie down in green pastures, he leads me beside quiet waters, he restores my soul.
REFLECT (10 min.)
RESPOND (10 min.)
REST (5 min.)

Day 2
READ (5 min.): Psalm 23:3b—He guides me in paths of righteousness for his name's sake.
REFLECT (10 min.)
RESPOND (10 min.)
REST (5 min.)

Day 3
READ (5 min.): Psalm 23:4—Even though I walk through the valley of the shadow of death,

I will fear no evil, for you are with me; your rod and your staff, they comfort me.
REFLECT (10 min.)
RESPOND (10 min.)
REST (5 min.)

Day 4
READ (5 min.): Psalm 23:5—You prepare a table before me in the presence of my enemies. You anoint my head with oil; my cup overflows.
REFLECT (10 min.)
RESPOND (10 min.)
REST (5 min.)

Day 5
READ (5 min.): Psalm 23:6—Surely goodness and love will follow me all the days of my life, and I will dwell in the house of the LORD forever.
REFLECT (10 min.)
RESPOND (10 min.)
REST (5 min.)

Prayer Tools: Meditation

Christian meditation is another method of prayer that has helped me, especially in the last two years, even though I began to practice it 25 years ago. Others have written on meditation using the terminology *the prayer of quiet, centering prayer,* or even *mysticism*, which is the academic term. It is also called contemplative prayer in Europe. Meditation is practiced by sitting in silence for 20 or 30 minutes twice per day, repeating a prayer word such as the name of Jesus, the Jesus Prayer, or a Scripture verse.

Rowan Williams states that meditation is not just one more thing to do. Contemplation is the only ultimate answer to this crazy world with its financial crises, advertising culture, and chaotic and unexamined emotions.

Below is the full quote from Dr. Rowan Williams, former Archbishop of Cantebury's Address posted in the Catholic Herald on Thursday, Oct. 11, 2012 by Cindy Wooden and given to the Synod of Bishops:

> *In this perspective, contemplation is very far from being just one kind of thing that Christians do: it is the key to prayer, liturgy, art and ethics, the key to the essence of a renewed humanity that is capable of seeing the world and other subjects in the world with freedom— freedom from self-oriented, acquisitive habits and the distorted understanding that comes from them. To put it boldly, contemplation is the only ultimate answer to the unreal and*

> *insane world that our financial systems and our advertising culture and our chaotic and unexamined emotions encourage us to inhabit. To learn contemplative practice is to learn what we need so as to live truthfully and honestly and lovingly. It is a deeply revolutionary matter.*

I learned much about the practice of meditation from Laurence Freeman in his seminar "Meditation is Pilgrimage." Much of the following material has been assimilated from what I learned at that seminar.

Keys to Meditation

Every person's journey in meditation is unique. Each author who has written on meditation carries a unique approach. They each have their own voice and their own experiences with God through meditation. This is encouraging to us because God made each of us uniquely and he will interact with us uniquely. So there are no formulas for meditation, though we can learn from the wisdom that others have learned through the centuries. There is freedom to intuitively know by our own experience how to do it. The important thing is to do it. You will learn what works well for you as you do it. Each of us will have a unique journey.

The first steps in meditation are ours. We engage in solitude and silence and set our minds upon the Lord. Focusing on our breathing is helpful. The last step is God's: He comes to meet with us, and it is a gift of grace. Attitude is important as we meditate. Bring a loving, adoring attitude to your prayer word or phrase. After all, you are sitting in the presence of your Creator God who loved us enough to redeem us after we went astray.

As you meditate, expect change to occur within. Rowan Williams says, "To be a contemplative as Christ is contemplative is to be open to all that Christ and the Father wish to call into our lives." Contemplation changes us. The change is for the glory of God: a human becoming more fully alive. The glory of God, revealed in us, means that we humans become fully alive. This growth glorifies God. The glory of God is reflected through us. Our unveiled faces reflect the glory of God—transparency of the truth in us is His glory. This should be true of our institutions and of us. This glorious change begins in us as we move into reality or into truth. With meditation, the teaching is free! Our attitude is different than the marketplace; so, don't approach meditation as if you are buying a product and will get something like peace or calmness. Instead, we are to pursue God, simply wanting to be with him experiencing his loving presence. Transformation comes as part of the package when we engage in meditation.

The nature of meditation mandates its being shared. If one tries to possess an experience, it will fade. At a certain point, you will want to share the experience. This is where community is important: you need to have a community of meditators to support each other in the practice or we might lose heart. The nature of God is community, a perfect communion of love. Our model is the Trinity, a community of three with Father, Son and Holy Spirit. As we begin to meditate, we also enter a great dynamic tradition. It is like a flowing river. The banks, representing the church, make it a river. The whole community or church transmits this wisdom. Just as we commune with the Trinity, we should also value the wisdom of believers who have gone before us and the community of believers we interact with daily. As we learn to reciprocate the gaze of the Father, then that inner experience becomes embodied as love for our neighbor. The pagans said in Bible times, "See how the Christians love each other." They are happy people. When they saw this love, they saw Christ.

Stages of Meditation

In the early church, they moved through three levels of contemplation:

1. Self-contemplation is when we become aware of our own demons such as anger, greed, pride, and laziness. We become aware of our own faults and failures. In this first stage, we try to become free from distortions of reality (fantasy).

2. Natural contemplation is less focused on "me" and more focused on seeing God in the world of nature. It provides religious people with new metaphors; the brain changes. We are embodied beings. We are creatures created by our Creator. It challenges us to live with the "unknowing": this is part of the contemplative journey. There is no

such thing as matter but instead energy and mass existing in relationship. Do we look at nature in an exploitive manner? We need "to see" it instead of "to look at" it.

3. The silent gaze of God is the third stage, which is contemplation in and of itself, existing of pure unconditional love. We enter the loving gaze of our Father and participate in true discipleship; we understand what it means to be a disciple of the Master. We are meant to go into it like a river flows into the ocean.

It may be helpful to you to explore each of these types of meditation. Try them out and see what works well for you. Turn your attention and heart to God, and He will meet with you as you meditate.

Meditation Grounds Us in Reality

The first challenge many people encounter when we begin our journey of contemplation is our high level of fantasy. We must go beyond fantasy to get to contemplation. We are encouraged in our world to live in a continuous state of fantasy. Stress thus increases because we are coming at our real issues from the viewpoint of fantasy not from truth.

When we leave fantasy and get into reality; that is when we can grow. The human grows in reality or truth. We must let go of the bad things that happen to us, and not keep wishing that they had not happened. They did happen! It is only in the real world that we can change. In meditation, we

195

accept the necessity to move out of fantasy into reality. Our foundation is Jesus, the Way, the *Truth*, and the Life.

In meditation, we make a commitment to stop fantasy. We learn to breathe under water: it is de-stressing. With meditation, we breathe the pure air of reality. People taste it and want more. Young people who engage in meditation often begin to *experience* the essence of what the church is before they *know* what it is.

The work of contemplation is to give pure attention. This is the self-forgetting gaze of love. In the Gospels, Jesus often looks at someone and loves him or her, like the encounter with the rich young ruler. In meditation, we allow Jesus to look at us as we look at Him. Meditation is primarily about the spiritual principle of attachment. Meditation facilitates a sense of reality that connects people to God. What is the nature of the Father? The essence of Jesus' purpose on earth was to show us the Father. Meditation creates a space for us to experience that connection.

The Father's gaze of love is the heart of reality! As we step outside of fantasy and focus our attention on the Father, we become grounded in reality as we ascend to communion with Him. This transformation is upsetting to the organization of our world. Once one bumps up against the real center of reality, we can never forget it. Jesus' gaze of love hits us at different times and at different levels.

The gaze of Jesus will find the weak spot in our defenses. We (in our fantasy) feel we are not safe! Jesus looks at us with compassion. He is faithful and he cannot be unfaithful to Himself. We will be healed and made whole if it is up to Him: and He is faithful to see us through.

When we experience His gaze, we are invited to return his gaze. If we don't, we will feel incomplete. We don't because we fear that we will cease to be: this is the ego facing its own transcendence. We begin coming up with conditions that are mean and petty. However, we can't make conditions with reality.

"Looking at" is different than "seeing." Perception of the person is possible with seeing. Seeing is the vision of God. Through meditation, we are transformed as we begin to truly see God and see ourselves. We find ourselves falling into a love relationship. The consequences of meditation and learning "to see" are uncontainable. They are experienced in our daily life. If we see God in this way, that seeing will change how we see each other.

The goal of meditation and seeking reality is not peace. Meditation can be misused as a religious form with a spiritual agenda. If our primary goal is peace and not communing with the Father, growth is arrested; it is like a railway spur going nowhere. This often happens when someone is meditating simply in order to relieve stress in order to have peace and not to connect with God. We want to simply connect with God in order to grow in our faith. Pope Francis says, "The carnival is over!" He is into simplicity. Following Jesus is simple, but not easy. Ironically, peace is often the byproduct but should not be the goal.

Julian of Norwich says, "Meditation is a state of complete simplicity costing everything!" The day is coming when the world will go mad. If there is a sane person, they will point at him and say that he is not like us. He is mad! They are thus taking sanity and turning it into something that is insane.

We must also let go of the attachment we feel to the pleasant feeling of meditation. In other words, we let go of using meditation as a form of escape. Meditation is about escaping from escapism into reality. Reality often involves pain. Meditation is one way to cope with grief as it allows you to go deeper into the feelings of loss. A great loss can be a great teaching! We must go into grief. It can open up wisdom, an insight, and a presence that we didn't have before. We learn from it even in the pain and through our pain.

Meditation has been a very life-giving tool for me to engage in prayer with God. It has become a daily practice for me, and it has brought great peace and calm into my life. As you learn to integrate meditation into your rhythm of life, you will walk in closer communion with God, and it will ground you in reality. The result will be a more restful and centered perception of your daily life and a more intimate attachment to the Father.

Prayer Tools: Journaling

Keeping a reflective journal may be one of the most important spiritual disciplines in my life to help me grow in relationships. What is especially helpful is the harvesting of my journal, which I do on retreats. Writing out your prayers in your journal and keeping a list of answered prayers is a helpful use of journaling also.

Since beginning in 1975, reflective journaling is the one spiritual discipline in my life that has stimulated the most spiritual growth. It has helped me tremendously in my relationships and especially in my marriage. I have been strongly influenced by Luci Shaw in her little book *Life Path*. Luci says the following about keeping a journal:

> *All kinds of words could be used to describe what keeping a reflective journal will do for the one who writes it; writing a journal regularly will enrich, nourish, mature, heal, develop, broaden, enhance, and transform you.*

No doubt about it, if you become a consistent journal keeper, you will change, or be changed as I have been. Below is a story from Luci's book on pages 13-15 which illustrates how a journal can be helpful in bringing healing to one's heart concerning a relationship.

> *Sharon Earl, a young married woman who spent a week with me in a journal workshop last summer wrote to me: "The first assignment you gave us, 'to write concretely and honestly,*

about a relationship,' had enormous impact for me. I decided to write about my sister who died in May. I felt I had dealt with my grief and did not feel particularly emotional as I began to write. I ended up writing my memories of her since her birth (she was four years younger than I.)

As I journaled (and journeyed) through her life I was shocked at the well of grief that gushed through me. I spent a good amount of time in deep, primal sobbing. I began to see patterns in my relationship to her that I hadn't noticed before, and areas of hurt that I'd been afraid to look at.

In my journal process I let myself consciously feel the lack of sister-closeness that pervaded our childhood. As her big sister, I often ignored her, occupied as I was with growing up and being with my own friends. Our four-year gap meant that when she was in high school, I was in college. When she was in college, I married. Our lives didn't really begin to cross until we both became mothers.

Soon after I became a mother, my husband and I left for Kenya with our child as missionaries. A month after our arrival, my husband died in an auto accident. For the next year, I was grieving, single-mothering, and healing. I also began dating my second husband, Shep. After we married, I became pregnant again when, BAM! the news of my sister's diagnosis of acute myoblastic leukemia hit me like a blow in the gut. I desperately wanted to be close to her, care for her, be there, make up for lost time,

*and claim the sisterhood that we should have
had. Slowly God began to redeem our
relationship in those final days, though my pain
distanced me at times. I gave her a mug that
said, "My Sister, My Friend," and meant it with
all my heart. Later Mom told me that my sister
had said, "That mug that Sharon gave me, the
sister mug, I wish I could take it to heaven." But
it was through this process of journaling that
God became more real for me, and I
experienced his healing and forgiveness."*

Personally, I can say that I began to grow spiritually when I began to keep a journal in 1975, 39 years ago at age 31. I was in a very low valley of my life, having been married for seven years with two children who were then age four and one. During the first seven years of our marriage, Peter had finished his last year of a university degree at Wheaton College followed by a three-year Masters of Divinity at TEDS in Chicago and a three-year doctoral program in England. I have said that during the first seven years of our marriage, all our time, energy, and money was poured into Peter Davids' head. I had taught school to support us, and then we became house parents at a private girls' high school, a job that fell primarily on me. He did his three-year doctoral program in England, and then we moved from England to Germany to begin missionary service. I was completely depleted of energy at that point in my life. I was physically ill, very lonely, trying to learn German, and experiencing culture shock. Our marriage relationship was very stressed. We were in transition.

During this transition, I began my first spiritual journal as a discipline—writing out Scripture verses in full that impacted me as I read them. I began on the first day to read Genesis 1, Psalm 1, and Matthew 1; thus, reading an Old Testament chapter, a Psalm, and a New Testament chapter every day. However, I began describing my life's emotional journey honestly at this time because I was so desperate. I was seeking God because I needed new life, new energy, renewed health, and overall refreshment. I had read a book with the above simple description of how to do a spiritual journal; so I tried it. Then I took a course on journaling later in 1983, which taught me a lot more that I will share with you. Below are some of the principles that I have learned about journaling.

Write About Your Feelings

Journal writing is a therapeutic tool. I often ask my counseling clients to do some writing as we work through their issues together. People often begin journals when they are going through transitions, when big change comes into their lives like the experience that I described above that was a major transition for me during which I began to journal.

The purpose of journal keeping is to get down on paper what you feel, helping you to reflect on your life journey. By the way, I realize that I am speaking as a baby boomer, so for you busters, net-gens, or cybergens, a journal can be kept on the computer. My husband, Peter, actually keeps his on his computer in Word. When he is on a trip, he writes on his iPad, which he can sync with his Mac. The purpose of a journal is to get down on paper or to record on screen with password protection what you feel.

A spiritual journal is written for yourself. Be honest! Do not write to share or your internal censorship bureau will spring into action to prevent a lot of important information and expression of feelings from emerging. If you are not honest, you are wasting your time, energy, and money. A journal is a place to air anxieties, to come in touch with your own reality with all honesty.

There is a mystery about putting words down on paper or up on a screen. The vague ideas running around in our heads become concrete in written words in our story. The mystery of the incarnation is bound up in this because Scripture says that Jesus is the Word of God that became flesh (John 1:14). Somehow, putting something into words is a mystery. With journaling, we partake in the mystery of incarnation.

Shaping of ideas happens on paper. Ideas remain vague unless expressed in words when they then seem to become concrete or clearer; they've come into the open or into the light. Having written something down, it is easier to share it later with a friend or remind yourself of your past or reflect upon it.

What a Journal Is and Isn't

Elizabeth O'Connor in her book *Letters to Scattered Pilgrims* says that there are some things that a journal is and some things that a journal is not.

First, a journal is *not:*

- *A daily dairy with a chronicle of events*, because your daily events need interpretation to know how you feel about them. Journaling involves reflection and interpretation.

- *An evidence of narcissism*, but a tool to aid in understanding self. For example, I was stuck in anger for two years, and journaling helped me see it and gave me perspective on how to begin to change. During a retreat, I asked myself three questions: where were you last year, where are you now, and where are you going next year? This reflection helped me understand myself. Then I wrote a summary answering each question in my journal.

- *An anti-social process*, but it is a tool to help you to be more social and relate better after reflecting upon your interpersonal communication in relationships.

- *A hunt for sin in your life.* It is not a place to be introspective, negative, faultfinding, condemnatory.

- *A substitute for prayer, devotional life, or professional therapy.* It is a reflective tool that might aid in all the above but not substitute for them.

♦ *A new legalism.* Rather than being something you must do, journaling is a gift that can help you grow.

♦ *A place to display writing skill.* It is a place to pour everything out on paper simply and honestly the way it comes tumbling out without hesitation or editing.

Second, a journal *is*:

♦ *A spiritual gift* wherein you take time to understand yourself.

♦ *A record* of the real you at a particular time and place.

♦ *A place* to record, understand, reflect, and/or get a new perspective.

♦ *A tool* by which to reorder life and set priorities.

♦ *A unifying instrument* by which to bring unity to life or bring simplicity to your complexity.

♦ *A place to record some memories.* An example is my father's death and funeral. My father died Nov. 7, 1999. His faith and my relationship to him are reasons that I became a missionary. In his book *Practicing the Presence of People* Mike Mason put it well:

> *Death, it is said, wonderfully concentrates the mind. Sadly and*

> *paradoxically, we never practice a*
> *person's presence so intently as*
> *when that one is gone. If only we*
> *could love in life as we do in death!*

I recognized after my dad's funeral, only after he was gone, what a huge hole he had left in my life and what a huge sphere of influence he had had over my life on every level. This reflection came as I journaled about our relationship after his funeral.

♦ *A place to make some decisions.* An example is a weighty decision Peter and I made in 2002. During February and March, I filled 200 pages with my musings over our decision to live in Bern, Vancouver, or Houston.

♦ *An aid to spiritual growth.* Bring your own outlook to life and to your decisions. You can discover your own voice and examine or shed light on your worldview by this process.

Guidelines for Journal Keeping

Some very practical tips will be useful to you as you begin your journaling journey. Begin by dating your entry. I keep track of my Bible reading just after the journal date at the top of the page and/or add a special holiday title or family event like a birthday. Before you start writing, take time to sit and wait. Center your thoughts and calm down. Then you can begin to write.

At a later time, go back and reread your journal entries. Do not change or edit it. If it would be helpful for future reads, you can write qualifications or explanations at the bottom and date these too, but don't change the entry itself. Rereading is called *harvesting your journal*. Harvesting my journal at the end of each year and writing a summary has been very helpful for me in sorting out my emotions and straightening out my relationships. In the harvesting process of summarizing and reflecting upon what I see, I discover truths and insights about myself that I never knew. I find a deep wisdom to guide my behavior.

On a practical note, keep your journal off the beaten path. Ask others not to read it, or password protect it, if kept on a computer. This, of course, is to ensure freedom to express your heart.

Another tip I've found helpful has come from Valerie Raoul:

> *A journal is always written in the present, and what is written becomes the record of the past, which you read in the future.*
>
> ~*Luci Shaw*, Life Path

Each of our lives is a journey with a beginning (the past) and an end (somewhere in the future) with the present sandwiched in between. The present represents where we are and the steps we are taking now. A journal helps us to follow and chart our life paths. There is a clear connection between journal keeping and journeying. Each speaks of the progress made in a day (the French word *jour* means day). Journal keeping is a daily record of your spiritual, emotional, intellectual, or artistic traveling, your personal edging closer to God, reality, true perception, and self-knowledge. Journaling is an opportunity to catch your life in words. One person has said that reflective writing encourages him to interact with himself as if he were an outsider. He gains a new perspective.

Sam Keen says:

To be alive is to have a past. We either repress the past and continue to fight its wars with new personnel, or we invite it into awareness so that we can see how it has shaped the present.

Elizabeth O'Connor explains that there are three tools for personal growth: reflection, self-observation, and self-questioning. She says that we are each on a pilgrim path, which is an inward journey of self-discovery. Self-knowledge is related to love and thus to God in this way. When we wake up to the truth in ourselves, we wake up to the Divine in us. The deepest, central part of ourselves is where God comes to dwell. Luke 17:20-21 says:

The Kingdom of God isn't ushered in with visible signs. You won't be able to say, "Here it is!" or "It's over there!" For the Kingdom of God is within you.

So it is within that we discover our self-worth, our heritage, and that we are sons and daughters of the Living God. He is the one who made us, sent us into the world, and will call us back to Him. Using the journaling tool helps us to take what is inside of us and place it outside of ourselves.

We can hold a piece of our life where we can look at it, meditate on it, deepen our understanding of it, and thus deepen our self-knowledge and understanding.

It is interesting to write what you see, especially if you are an artistic type. Allow your senses to inform what to write. Springtime certainly is a great time to do this with new life bursting out all around us. Maybe you want to sketch in your journal or write your poems or your dreams. What would be important for you to record in your journal? How have you chronicled your life?

Another way is to write God a letter or to write a dialog between you and God. An interesting thing to do in a journal is to write out a Scripture passage from your perspective and see what turns up; how does God speak to you through the exercise? Paraphrase the portion to see if you understood it by writing it in your own words.

Journal keeping is a form of prayer; we are searching our hearts in God's presence and asking him to know our thoughts. Luci Shaw has said that the voice of God is like a small bird; if you want it to light on your shoulder you must stand very still. Then perhaps we must write down what He says quickly to remember it. Journaling is a way to reflect on your life and chronicle the events to discern purpose and meaning. There are many ways to keep a journal, so seek the way that best suits your own personality. What fits in with your life style, your worldview, or your way of doing things?

Types of Journals

In his book *A Book of One's Own* Thomas Mallon describes seven types of diaries, as he calls them: chroniclers, travelers, pilgrims, creators, apologists, confessors, and prisoners. Mallon explains that the diary has an audience in mind; most often it is the true person down inside. Sometimes, we are saying: "I was, I was--- I am"! It is interesting to discover which type above represents your style. Here is a small description of each for you to see which one most nearly describes what you might do if you were to keep a journal or have been keeping one for years.

Chroniclers write about everything: the everyday occurrences, the exciting events, the boring, the interesting, the fascinating, the melancholy private thoughts, as well as general public opinions. They write to collect the days. Virginia Woolf says her fundamental motive is to hold on to it all, to chart the clock and death of all the things that she had lived. A diary entry on October 7, 1919: "I wonder why I do it? Partly, I think, from my old sense of the race of time. Time's winged chariot hurrying near; does it stay?" The chronicler values every day as exceptional and celebratory enough to commemorate.

Travelers value their trip as a special set of days to commemorate. Visitor's books are the diaries which travelers keep for places and represent the reverse of the impulse that causes travelers to keep diaries for themselves: namely, to take a piece of a foreign place back with them. The telephone has killed letter writing, whereas the camera has dealt a severe blow to a travel diary. Some people still do it to say that this is what I, not the Nikkon, recorded. Earliest travel diaries were kept mainly for geography. Travelers preserve impressions of foreign places, thus learning about themselves and their world by contrast to others and to their worlds. Lewis and Clark kept great travel journals of their explorations.

Pilgrims are serious individuals who set out in their diaries to discover their true selves. They are out to find God and reach their full potential as persons in every aspect but especially in the spiritual aspect. Some are sorrowful souls carrying great burdens. Henry Thoreau discovered and manufactured a self. He sought in his journals to comprehend the world, to simplify and perfect his place in it.

Creators keep a commonplace book of their readings and thoughts, which go into their art. Sometimes other people in their lives keep these books like Dorothy Wordsworth kept this book for her brother, William. This notebook serves as a record of the message between the inspiration and the art. Mary Shelley's journals kept records of readings for her husband. The artists have ultimately been most concerned to let their final creations, rather than their notebooks, do their talking to posterity.

Apologists write their story down in a journal to explain to the world what actually took place in their life. Politicians often keep this kind of diary. Apologists want to make history prick up its ears and take notice, however briefly. Examples of apologist journal-keepers include Richard Nixon and Lee Harvey Oswald.

Confessors use their journal to confess their secrets. The confessional diary can announce "I was wrong" with as much insistence as the apologists proclaims "I was right". Having been brought to life by the dour Puritans of the seventeenth century, the diary in the preceding 200 years was a place in which the faithful might privately expiate their sins; but by the late nineteenth century the diary had become more typically the place in which they could savor them. The apologia is directed towards posterity and the confessional might be, but it is just as likely to be a matter between the writer and God or the writer and his or her conscience. The confessional diary is a very pliable priest. It keeps the secret. This secrecy animates the confessional diary beyond all others. The secret-keeping adolescent diary is, or certainly has been, pre-eminently a female genre. The little girl may be being trained in dailiness. Examples of this type are a criminal, as seen in Dorian Gray and a female adolescent, and a great psychoanalysis, as seen in Karen Horney.

Prisoners actually live their lives in their diaries. It becomes "the world" for these individuals. They look for a place to come alive and find it in the diary. The diary becomes substitution, sublimation, or transference. An example is Captain Alfred Dreyfus, a French Jewish officer who was falsely accused, exiled to a prison island, and then exonerated. Other examples include Anne Frank, the young

Jewish girl; Albert Speer, Hitler's master architect; and Joshua Naples who shoveled in graveyards, operating with a gang of body snatchers for doctors and schools of anatomy.

I've discovered that my later style is that of a pilgrim mainly who is seriously searching for the true person inside, seeking to understand myself through journal writing. But there are bits of several of the above types in me. My main beginning style was that of the chronicler for I wanted to journal everyday, catching the essence or the uniqueness of my day. I've lived all over the world and have wanted to catch the essence of each culture in which I've lived. Since I've been a counselor/teacher/writer, I've creatively kept significant quotes in my journal to which I later wanted to refer. I also found myself as a teenage girl keeping my secrets in my diary while I locked and hid the key. I've found traces of five of the seven different styles in my journal keeping over the last 50 years as I've matured and journeyed down the road. Where do you find yourself in the types above?

Journaling Methods

Hearn's Method

Instead of keeping the journal in one book, another method is Virginia Hearn's style of journal keeping, patterned after Ira Progoff's *At a Journal Workshop* with ten sections for the journal, kept in a loose-leaf binder. The sections are:

1. Soul Country
2. Period Log
3. Daily Log
4. Stepping Stones
5. Dialogue with the Body
6. Dialogue with Persons
7. Unsent Letters
8. Free-flow Writing - art & music
9. Dialogue with God
10. Dream Log

In the *Soul Country* section, you might deal with questions like what time is it in my life? What is ahead? What do I want to accomplish in my life? Who are the people in my soul country? What message do I want to send each one of them? We might deal with comments on artifacts of an early 21st century female and the significance of each one of them. Thoughts to begin a journal entry might include "Because I am a woman . . ." or "Sense bridges from here to the world out there . . . "

The *Period Log* sees yourself now, between the past and the future. You ask and write about questions such as: What led up to this period? What am I doing with my life, work, school, projects, and commitments? What relationships are important and why? How is my health? What social groups am I in? Have there been any big events or inner experiences? What metaphor would I use to describe this period? What would surprise other people if they knew? This is a dialogue with my history. What musings do I have about my spouse, children, grandchildren, or siblings?

The *Daily Log* is not a laundry list or a tabulation of today. Relax and ask yourself these questions: What was important today? What am I feeling about today? What are my big concerns right now?

The *Stepping Stones* are the milestones or very important events of your life. Milestones include significant times in your life, and sometimes the milestones are very different from other times. Who are the important people behind each stepping-stone?

Dialogue with the Body is a reflection on how our aspirations, emotions, motives, and so on are carried out by the body. The body makes our contact with the world. The body is unique. We are often concerned about our appearance but not the inner workings of the body. We can write out our stepping-stones of the body or write a dialogue with the body in this section.

Dialogue with Persons is a place to reflect on the significance of a person in your life. First, list the person and make a brief factual statement about them. Then perhaps write a stepping stone portion about them. Allow the person to appear in your mind's eye and write a dialogue with them. It is like play, going back and forth.

Me:

Person:

Me:

Person:

This does not have to be with a person near you or a person who is alive. Do a series of personal dialogues with time intervals in between them and observe how the dialog changes over time. You can even personify things and dialogue with them.

Unsent letters is a section in our journal where we can work out struggles in our relationships, such as when a close relationship has ended, a problem arises in a relationship, or a past situation in a relationship is not yet settled. In this section, write a letter to this person and first explain the situation as you recall it. Then state your point of view and the other person's point of view. We can tell the other person whether reconciliation is possible from your point of view and figure out steps to take in that direction.

Free-Flow Journaling is training in awareness. It should be calming. This can involve art and music. Take a beautiful object or sculpture, sit in front of it, and look at it for five minutes. Do not think, but record your musings. You can do the same thing with a painting or a piece of music.

Dialogue with God is a place to record your spiritual journey. Write your spiritual stepping stones. Record your conversation with God, or write a letter to Him. Write out your prayers.

Dream Log is a place to reflect on your dreams. Record dreams in series. Sense the major feeling in each dream. After a while, themes emerge. Generally, the interpretation is individual, meaning that it applies to your life.

Shaw's Method

Here is yet another method to keep a journal, and it is the one I personally follow. Luci Shaw's method of writing a journal is as a whole, not divided into a spiritual journal, a journal of events, or any other separation of sacred and secular. No thing is inappropriate for a journal with this method. We need to have freedom to keep our journal in whatever way suits us best. Luci talks about putting quotes from books she is reading at the back of her journal. I actually put these quotes right into the daily journal entry with an interpretive comment as to why the quote is important to me. I put special birthday cards, brochures, and keepsakes into my journal to decorate it. It all flows together with my prayers and reflections on life and relationships.

How to Begin

How do you begin? First, gather the simple tools with which to journal: something on which to write and something with which to write, like paper and a pen. Or, if you are from a later generation than I, you will need your computer and a program in which to write; my husband uses his Mac with Word.

Choosing a journal carefully may be important because this may subtly shape the ease with which you write, what you write, and the way you write it. Somewhere between respect for yourself and the freedom you need to write will determine what kind of journal you choose in which to express yourself: a beautifully bound book, loose-leaf notebook, tape recorder, computer, iPhone, or iPad.

After choosing a journal and getting started, establish a daily rhythm and maintain this discipline in your life. Take advantage of the gift of writing in your journal each day. Then to get maximum good from this process, periodically harvest your journal.

Harvesting Your Journal

It is important to occasionally harvest your journal by going back and reading it, reflecting on its content, and then writing a summary of where you have been in that past period of time. I do this once per year.

To harvest your journal, take the following steps:

1. Take a spiritual retreat
2. Re-read your journal
3. Write a summary answering each of the three questions below.
   - Where have I been?
   - Where am I now?
   - Where am I going? The answer here will be your goals for the New Year. You might even want to make a plan to carry out your new goals, stating what steps you need to take to get what you want.

A friend of mine did this recently, and she discovered a hidden truth that had put pressure on her marriage for the last 20 plus years. She had always thought that she had wanted to plant a church and had put pressure on her husband to do so. Upon rereading her journals, she discovered that her real personal goal was working in pastoral ministry among women, children, and others in her circle of relationships. In her original denomination, the only way a woman could minister as she wanted to do was to be the pastor's wife, so she had insisted that her husband plant a church and become a pastor so she could be the pastor's wife and carry out her goals. This was not his heart or his calling.

When she discovered this about herself, she told him about her reflective discovery. Since they were then in a new church where she had freedom as a woman to minister, she can minister to her heart's desire. She may never have known this and been able to take the pressure off her marriage unless she had harvested her journal.

Another story about the benefit of harvesting the journal is so very important to me, because it is my story. I was angry with Peter for two whole years, and I did not even know it. The way I discovered this astonishing marriage relational fact was by harvesting my journals. I was in the habit of making an annual hermitage retreat for one week all by myself in a cabin by the sea in Sechelt, British Columbia.

On these retreats, I tried to practice as many spiritual disciplines at once that I could, like fasting or praying without ceasing in the silence and solitude of the beautiful Pacific Ocean's pebble beach on which my cabin was located, nestled in among the huge evergreen trees that lined the shore. To harvest my journals, I would take the entries from the previous entire year and read through them on the first evening of my retreat. Then I would write a one-page summary answering the first of three important direction-finding questions: where was I during this past year? I would go to sleep musing on this question. The next morning I would write a second one-page summary in my journal answering the question, where am I now? Then I would spend the rest of the week walking on the beach and talking with God asking myself the last question: where are we going this next year, God? At the end of the week I would write a one-page summary of the new goals the Lord had shown me that I needed to make for the next year.

During this particular revelatory retreat, my journals from the year before began with a summary from the previous year, so I first read that and then read through the journals from the whole year. I wrote my one-page summary asking myself where I had been during the last year. The next morning, I got up to write in my journal a second summarizing page of where I was now, but I first reread the last year's summary that I had written the night before. I suddenly realized that it sounded very similar to the summary of the previous year. I placed these two yearly summaries side by side and reread them both. I was astounded at how tragically similar both summaries were. They both commented on my being very angry with my husband Peter. It was at that moment that I realized I was stuck in anger in my marriage relationship and that I had remained this way for two fiery years. I would not have seen this if I had not been journaling honestly about my relationships and if I had not harvested my journals to glean reflective truths about my relationships and myself.

At that moment, I was reminded of the Bible verse that says we should not let the sun go down on our anger. Many suns (maybe as many as 730) had gone down on my anger at Peter, and I had been daring to wonder why I was not happy in my marriage relationship. So I got up as I finished my reflections in my journal and took a long walk on the beach and asked God and myself what we were going to do about this problem. At low tide, I sat down on my favorite huge rock which I had nick-named the giant's hand because it had grooves worn in it by the ocean's waves which looked like huge knuckles. I stared up into the sky and angrily asked God if there was one good reason to love Peter Davids. Immediately out of the blue came the powerful question, "Could you love him for me?" Oh, wow, did that question cut to the quick of my heart; for it was the only way that I could have imagined answering yes to God in that stuck place where I was in my relationship with my husband. I felt as if I were knocked backward by the force of this question and plastered to the rock. I was stunned! I did immediately answer God with these words, "Yes, I choose to love Peter for you. That is the only way I possibly could."

During the week, Father God instructed me that I also needed to forgive Peter for the hurt he had caused me so that I could be free to love him. I cried many tears and confessed my sin of holding onto my anger in unforgiveness. I allowed the Holy Spirit to bring comfort to my soul as He washed over me with his forgiveness and assurance of His love. I had the time to creatively imagine with the help of the Holy Spirit during that week how I could walk out the truth that I had seen with the aid of harvesting my journal that year. Basking in His love and forgiveness, I was enabled to forgive and choose to love once again. So, at the end of the week, I wrote a one-page summary of my relational goals. I would go on to check these goals the next year to see if I had grown.

Keeping and harvesting a spiritual journal led to much spiritual growth in my relationships, especially bringing light into my marriage relationship. For these personal reasons, I highly recommend the spiritual exercise of keeping a reflective journal: it aids spiritual growth in one's soul.

Journaling Exercises

Try this exercise I call "What time is it in my life?" Take a blank piece of paper or your journal, and at the top of the page, draw a clock without hands on it.

First, ask yourself the question, what time is it in my life? Then put the hands on your clock, telling the time in the following ways. Write one or two descriptive sentences such as my life is standing still, this is a lonely time, this is a time of new beginnings, or this is a challenging and exciting time in my life.

Second, answer the question, what does it mean to me to be in this time of my life?

Third, what color describes this time?

Fourth, what sounds are in my life? What adjectives describe my life: fast, slow, exciting, boring, interesting, busy, challenging, scary, safe, peaceful, harried, chaotic, fulfilling, frustrating, or other?

Fifth, how do I feel about this time of my life?

Sixth, what people or events are in my life at the moment?

Seventh, what are the milestones in my life, perhaps by decades?

Last, ask yourself, how long has this time lasted? Is this the beginning, the middle, or the end of a chapter?

You might want to think of your clock with four quarters. The top right between the numbers 12:00 and 3:00 represent the years 0-20 or spring. The bottom right quarter between 3:00 and 6:00 represent the years 21-40 or summer. The bottom left quarter between 6:00 and 9:00 perhaps are the years 41-60 or fall. The top left quarter between 9:00 and 12:00 could represent the years 61 to death or winter.

What time is it in my life? A proverb says we are born to die. A Bible verse found in Ecclesiastes 7:4 says that the wise person thinks much on death. Ecclesiastes also says earlier that "the day you die is better than the day you were born." So, it might do well to think about what time it is in your life. Where are the clock's hands on your life time clock? Maybe you can draw them in now or adjust them after answering these questions if you have not already have done so. What time is it?

Below are some other journaling exercises to try out at a later date.

1. Do a stepping-stones exercise. Draw some big stones on your paper and write meaningful milestones of your life on each one and the significance thereof.

2. Do a dialogue with God, with "God" and "me" talking back and forth in your script.

3. Read Psalm 136 responsively. Be a reflective person! Write out your own psalm (with thanksgiving) in the pattern of this Psalm, using the history of your own life between the verses of gratitude.

You may want to do some reading on journaling if it is new to you. Or you may want to begin again if you used to do it and have left it out of your life lately. You will find a bibliography at the end, if you are interested in further reading.

Play: Becoming Energized and Restored

There is a kind of play we can engage in that restores our soul. Much of what we do for entertainment is simply "zoning out." I zone out playing Solitaire or looking at Facebook on the computer. Many people zone out in front of a TV. Play and leisure is meant to leave us energized and restored.

Each of us needs to discover how to play in such a way that it will refresh our own soul. Examples of play include gardening, hitting the yard sales early on a Saturday morning, playing the piano, knitting, fishing, having friends over for dinner, reading a good novel, bicycling, playing tennis, swimming, bowling or simply taking long walks outdoors.

The aspect that separates work from play is not so much the activity itself; rather, it is your reason for doing it. If you are doing an activity in order to make a living, or for someone else, then it is called work. If you are doing the activity simply because you enjoy it, then it is called play. Learning how to play is not as easy as it sounds. I love this example of learning to play by my friend Charles Bello:

> Growing up, I loved to draw. As a child I would draw for hours. Over the years this practice was reduced to doodling on scratch paper while having boring and life-draining conversations

227

*over the telephone. A number of years ago, I
returned to doing pen-and-ink drawings. When
I initially started drawing again, I felt this
strange pressure to do it for others. In other
words, I felt this inner drive to draw well, so
that others would think that I was a good
artist. Play had become work once again.
Through prayer and intense inner work, I was
able to return to the place where I can draw
simply for myself because I enjoy it and it feeds
my soul.*

*Another way that I play is to take long walks in
nature. I know that there are health benefits in
regular walking, but I don't walk for those
reasons (that would be called exercise). I walk
because it feeds my soul and because I enjoy
seeing what God has created. It is a divine
waste of time; and therefore, this play is very
refreshing.*

Our culture pushes us to put a utilitarian value on
everything. We approach our friendships, our church
affiliation, our relationship to nature, and even our play as
having value in as much as it contributes to work and helps
us to be successful. We used to play tennis, now we "work
on our serve."

When I was a little girl, I played by skipping jump
rope outdoors or riding my bicycle. Now, I bicycle each
morning to keep in shape and there is no element of play in
it. It feels like work.

Play within the context of sabbatical rhythm is meant
to help us slow down, enjoy our life, and find rest. We are to

find rest not only for our bodies, but for our minds as well. Leland Ryken writes, "Any leisure activity will become just another form of work if pursued with the compulsion of work."

It is up to you to discover how to play in a way that honors God and feeds your soul. What might look like play to me, may be work for you. My friend Brian loves to cook Thai and Indian food. His wife is presently going to college, and he is now doing much of the daily meal preparation for his family. The daily meals are work, but occasionally he invites some close friends over for Thai food, which he loves to cook. This is play for him. Work is what you have to do; play is what you want to do.

God used the contemplative prayer model of the Examen to get me in me touch with my playful self again. I must also confess that I needed to develop a theology for playing so I could play without guilt. I had such a strong and warped work ethic that I had a difficult time making play a priority in my life. Ryken's book *Redeeming the Time: A Christian Approach to Work & Leisure* was really beneficial in helping me find a balance.

This is very basic stuff, but many of us live as though we don't know it. Often we don't *do it* even though we do know it. We ignore it or forget it. So, I remind you again today. We need a Sabbath Rhythm of pause, pray, and play in our lives. Begin now!

Ruth Haley Barton in her book, An Invitation to Solitude and Silence, says that Sabbath keeping is "a way of ordering one's entire life to honor the creation rhythm of things—work and rest, waking and sleeping, seriousness for survival and playfulness for refreshment, fruitfulness and dormancy as in the seasons, giving and receiving, birth and death, words and silence, being and doing, activism and surrender. There is something deeply spiritual about honoring these limitations of our human existence as created beings. We are physical and spiritual beings in a world of time and space. A peace comes when we accept reality rather than always pushing beyond our limits, trying to play God. There is a freedom that comes from being who we are in God and resting in God. This eventually enables us to bring something truer to our life than all that our driven-ness brings."

Sabbath keeping helps us to live within our limits because on the Sabbath, in so many different ways, we allow ourselves to be the creature in the presence of our Creator, we allow ourselves to be a child in the presence of its Father, and we allow our relationships with Him to take priority and we allow ourselves to become refreshed with play. We touch something more real than what we are able to produce on our own. We touch that deep place inside us where the Holy Spirit meets our spirit and we come to life.

So how will you act today to put a rhythm of work and rest—engaging in the spiritual battle and then retreating—into your life? How will you place in your life the principle of keeping a Sabbath Rhythm so you can run the race well to its final end? How will you place spiritual exercises into your life to keep yourself in love with God and connected to Him and keep yourself from burning out?

I challenge you to reflect on your life, to balance work and rest, to place the appropriate needed spiritual disciplines into your life in order to place yourself in God's way and stay connected to Him in order to grow: pause, pray, and play.

Community Building

Alongside the lessons of pause, pray, and play, the concept of community had a large place in my healing process. I read about it in a book called *The Different Drum: Community Making and Peace* written by Scott Peck, a psychiatrist who had worked for the US Army. This reading had a profound impact on me. A blurb on the front cover calls the book "A Spiritual Journey Toward Self-Acceptance, True Belonging, and New Hope for the World." One commentator says that Peck's challenge is to achieve, through the creative experience of community, a new connectedness and wholeness. I learned how Peck had created an emotionally safe community that he thought would bring global peace. I realized that his method of creating community was the same way that I had already created a safe place in recovery groups for sexually abused women. This encouraged me that I also could do this in a group of weary pastors. There is a challenge at the end of Peck's book, which I took to heart: start a community wherever you are on this earth and win the "war against peace" with love.

Right on the heels of reading this book by Peck, I read of two more ways to create community and friendship. The first was through a Christian psychologist, Larry Crabb, in two of his books called *The Safest Place on Earth* and *Connected*. Crabb presented through a Christian hermeneutic what Peck had said in a more inclusive secular way, even though Peck was a Christian. The second way I discovered for creating community was in an article by a Malaysian friend who talked about Henri Nouwen's book *With Burning Hearts*. This article by Soo Inn Tan said that Christian ministry has an order: communion, community, and ministry. (I've found it easier to remember these three elements with the alliteration "communion, community, and commission.") So we must have communion with the Trinity, community with our brothers and sisters, and then commission to the whole world as we do our ministry. Omitting the second step of community will kill us because we do not have any support for our ministry or for ourselves.

I realized that before my burnout I had been ministering in that way with my counseling, skipping the critical second step of community. As I read these three groups of authors, I decided to work relationally and put the community step back into my ministry. I made a decision right then and there that when we moved to Houston, I would work in this new community-building method. I planned retreats for pastors but built in this concept of community with the principles of recovery from the recovery movement. I have since learned through experience that the development of community is vital to the healing process.

Definitions of Community

To understand what is meant by this concept, let us look at some definitions of community by various authorities on the subject. Included in this section are definitions of community by educator Parker Palmer, North Carolina pastor Jim Kallum, psychiatrist Scott Peck, Christian psychologist Larry Crabb, and Malaysian Baptist pastor Soo Inn Tan.

Parker J. Palmer's definition of a learning community has caught my attention from his little book, *To Know as We Are Known: A Spirituality of Education*. Palmer contrasts the image for a therapeutic community with two other images. True therapeutic community requires a capacity for open, vulnerable relationships so that psychological wounds can be revealed and healed, wherein community equals intimacy.

Palmer's first contrasting image is a civic community, which is about the relations of strangers who will never know each other well but who must learn to hang together lest they hang separately. The goal of a civic community is to learn how to compromise, and the norm for relationships is one of tolerance and civility.

Palmer also talks about the second contrasting image as an education community, which he says is a community where knowing, teaching, and learning are at its heart. Palmer states,

> *Real learning does not happen until students are brought into relationship with the teacher,*

> *with each other, and with the subject. We*
> *cannot learn deeply and well until a community*
> *of learning is created in the classroom.*

Palmer talks about three important disciplines in a learning community: study, prayer, and gathering.

> *In the gathered life of the spiritual community,*
> *I am brought out of the solitude of study and*
> *prayer into the discipline of community and*
> *relatedness. The community is a check against*
> *my personal distortions; it helps interpret the*
> *meaning of texts and gives guidance in my*
> *experience of prayer. But life in community is*
> *also a continual testing and refining of the*
> *fruits of love in my life. Here, in relation to*
> *others, I can live out (or discover I am lacking)*
> *the peace and joy, the humility and*
> *servanthood by which spiritual growth is*
> *measured. The community is a discipline of*
> *mutual encouragement and mutual testing,*
> *keeping me both hopeful and honest about the*
> *love that seeks me, the love I seek to be.*

So Palmer talks about a spiritual community that sounds in my estimation very similar to the church, and his goals for the education community, as he describes it, are goals we should ascribe to in Christian community.

A fuller picture of community emerges as one looks at the definition of church from a North Carolinian pastor named Jim Kallum:

> *The church is to be a community, a safe place*
> *that provides a vision for people and wisdom*
> *for living life. It is to be a place that allows*

power to be released, enabling believers to struggle with life.

Kallum explains that community has four components:

1. Safety—"Accept me!"
   There is nothing that you could ever say or do that would cause me to walk away! (Zephaniah 3:9-20).
2. Vision—"Believe in me!" This vision is the ability to view me with a commitment to realize who I can become.
   I do accept you but I want more for you (Galatians 4:19, Colossians 1:28, 29).
3. Wisdom—"Challenge me!"
   Wisdom will challenge what needs to change so Christ can be seen more fully (Hosea).
4. Power—"Pour into me!" Releasing the internal power source of the Spirit.
   It is never about my maturity but about our maturity (Ephesians 3: 14-19).

Community involves risk and it runs counter-culture. Jim Kallum crashed after trying to pastor a church in his own steam for 18 years. He spent time with God in the wilderness and learned many lessons and came back saying the above about church.

Scott Peck's material also greatly encouraged me in my quest for understanding community in a more healthy way. Peck's book challenged me to work in this way of community building every time I build a new group or do a new ministry.

According to Peck, the true meaning of community can be defined in this way:

> *Community is restricted to a group of individuals who have learned how to communicate honestly with each other, whose relationships go deeper than their masks of composure, and who have developed some significant commitment to "rejoice together, mourn together," and to "delight in each other, make others' conditions their own."*

Community is something bigger than us and it is mysterious. It is miraculous. It is unfathomable. It can only be explained by explaining its parts, like a beautiful gem that can only be explained by describing its many facets. However, it is so exquisitely beautiful that the concept might seem unreal or unattainable or absurdly Utopian. The seeds of community reside in humanity, a social species: the picture here of community in the rough is like a gem in the rough, which we call a stone.

Peck goes on to describe these facets that make up the gem of community. They are interconnected, profoundly interrelated. No one could exist without the other. They create each other; make each other possible. What follows, then, is but one scheme for isolating and naming the most salient characteristics of a true community:

1. *Inclusivity, commitment, and consensus—*
   Community must be inclusive: there is an "all-

ness" in the community process on all levels including different sexes, races, creeds, emotions, and styles. Community can be described as a group that has learned to transcend its individual differences. Transcend means climbing over, and community is a group's having reached a mountaintop. It is a place where differences are appreciated. It requires a firm commitment to each other to do this as well. Consensus is another part of the community process that is almost mystical or magical. It cannot be described, only experienced where each member comes independently to the same conclusion.

2. *Realism*—A group has such a wide perspective that a more realistic decision can be reached. Humility is an important ingredient of a community as well.

3. *Contemplation*—A community is constantly examining itself, reflecting on its life together. Meekness is a part of community and this is a true knowing and feeling of a man's self as he is. This is almost a contemplative spirit in a real community.

4. *A safe place*—Community involves a place where one can be himself or herself and be accepted and share his or her own story without fear of rejection. A truly emotionally safe place is a healing atmosphere.

5. *A laboratory for personal disarmament*—In community, we see each other with soft eyes while dropping judgments, prejudices, distrust, fear, and resentment. These attitudes are replaced by love and trust.

6. *A group that can fight gracefully*—Community is a safe place where conflicts can be resolved without physical or emotional bloodshed and with wisdom as well as grace. Members have become skilled at listening and understanding, where they respect each others' gifts and accept each others' limitations, where they celebrate their differences and bind each others' wounds, where they are committed to a struggling together rather than against each other.

7. *A group of all leaders*—There is a flow of leadership shared by all. The spirit of community itself leads; not any single individual.

8. *A spirit of peace and love*—Quietness descends on the group and the atmosphere is so peaceful and gentle as a group enters into real community.

Peck also describes stages that communities experience. Community is never stagnant; it is constantly evolving. These are the stages of community making Peck has identified.

1. *Pseudocommunity*—A group tries to fake community in the beginning by being polite, kind, and well-mannered with each other. It is

240

pretense, an inviting but illegitimate shortcut to nowhere. The members allow each other to get away with blanket statements: this is a denial of individual differences.

2. *Chaos*—This stage always centers on well-intentioned but misguided attempts to heal and convert. Individual differences are right out in the open. Sometimes members bash each other over the heads with their differences trying to convert each other and make everyone normal. It is a time of fighting and struggle. The response to a group in chaos is often despairing: the struggle is going nowhere, accomplishing nothing. It is no fun. The group often not only attacks each other but also the leader.

3. *Emptiness*—There are only two ways out of chaos. One way is into organization, which is not community, and the other way is into emptiness. A group needs to empty themselves of barriers to communication. This emptiness includes emptying oneself of the following barriers:

   • Expectations and preconceptions—Because community is a scary adventure, we humans usually fill our minds with expectations and preconceptions of what it should be like. Then we try to force it to be that way which is usually destructive. Until such time as we can empty ourselves of expectations and stop trying to fit others and our relationships with them into a preconceived mold we cannot really listen, hear, or experience.

- Prejudices—These are the judgments we make of people when we have no or little experience with them.

- Ideology, theology, and solutions or any idea that assumes the status of the one and only right way—We need to take the stance of a learner in humility with a sense of humor.

- The need to heal, convert, fix, or solve—This is usually a self-centered desire for comfort through the obliteration of these differences. There may be a better way of appreciation and celebration of interpersonal differences.

- The need to control—The desired outcome of community must be the creation of a group as a whole, not that of an authoritarian leader who calls the shots. This emptiness is like dying: the group is dying.

4. *Community*—True community is formed when the group has finished dying: a soft quietness descends upon it. It is a kind of peace that bathes the entire room. One member will begin talking quietly and the whole group hangs on every word. The group has become one or a real community. It is like falling in love.

Peck's definition and explanation of community takes my breath away. It seems like a little bit of heaven so to speak. Notice that safety and discernment are part of both Peck's and Kallum's package. Scott Peck has discussed what Palmer might call a therapeutic community or what several of the others call church or a spiritual community.

Larry Crabb describes a spiritual community in terms of the messages a community communicates. The four messages of a spiritual community are:

1. *We accept you*—We celebrate your purity in Christ as we *worship God.* (Members have a new purity.)
2. *We believe in you*—We envision your new identity in Christ and what you can become, as we *trust God.* (Members have a new identity.)
3. *We see you and are glad to stay involved*—We discern your good passions and delight in them; we discern your bad passions and know that they do not define you, as we ourselves continue to *grow in Christ.* (Members have a new disposition.)
4. *We give to you*—We apply no pressure to change you. The power to change is already in you. We give you what is most alive in us with the prayer that it will set you free to indulge your deepest desires as we eagerly *obey God.* (Members have new power.)

Three of these messages are very similar to Jim Kallum's definition, if you recall. Accepting someone the way they are, believing in them, and caring for them are important elements of community no matter what brand of community you ascribe to.

My Malaysian Baptist pastor friend by the name of Soo-Inn Tan quotes Henri Nouwen from his little book *With Burning Hearts* and tells us that ministry has an order of communion, community, and commission. This involves communion with our Father God in our vertical relationship, community with our brothers and sisters in our horizontal relationships, and commission or ministry to the globe or to whomever on the globe God sends us to minister. We very often want to jump from communion with God straight to ministry leaving out community in which relationships we find our human support and companionship. God sent us out two by two, knowing we need community to minister.

In fact, many of our emotional needs are met as we belong to a group and find support in a safe community. Dennis and Shelia and Matthew Linn share some key thoughts on this point in their book *Belonging: Bonds of Healing and Recovery*. They state that belonging is created by the four parts of affirmation, taken from pages 97-105 of their book and summarized here:

1. *Knowing our own goodness*—We can affirm others only to the extent that we have received affirmation ourselves and know our own goodness. What matters most is whether people are connected to their real selves and know their goodness. I have learned from 12-step groups

that sometimes those who outwardly look like the most wounded, messiest people are the most healed, because they have learned to be real. Thomas Aquinas said that humility presumes greatness. In other words, human beings are great. The reason we need humility is to keep our greatness or goodness in perspective, lest we think we are better than God or other people. But if we were not good, we would not need humility.

2. *Noticing goodness*—The second part of the movement of affirmation, which creates belonging, is to notice goodness wherever we find it. As we notice goodness, it notices us and reflects back to us our own goodness. We can begin anywhere, because the same presence of God fills all created things. Sheila Linn states, "If I can notice the goodness in a tree or in a stone, I am more open to the goodness in others and in myself. Thus, reconnecting with the universe helps me belong to myself, others, and God. As a child, I could stare at a blade of grass noticing how utterly good it was and sense that a presence was looking back at me and I felt connected inside. It seemed that presence was noticing how good I was and trying to tell me that I was loved, that I belonged. I sensed this goodness in Christians and that is how I, Sheila, a Jewess became a Christian. Somehow early in life I had

sensitivity to the presence of God in all things, and it is one way I took in healing love. Now I try to live that way consciously."

3. *Being moved by goodness*—When someone does notice our goodness or when we notice it in another, the third part of the movement of affirming love that creates belonging is to be moved by that goodness—to feel joy and delight in it, without seeking to possess, use or change the other. Look at the faces of healthy parents as they gaze at their newborn babe: they exhibit pure delight that this child exists. However, we cannot convey spontaneous delight in one another unless we can feel all our emotions. Our emotions are connected, and if we repress one the others will not function properly either. As I become friendlier with all of my emotions, my capacity to be moved by the goodness of others grows. The more I am delighted by the goodness around me, the more of it I notice, and the more I sense it noticing me and reflecting back to me my own goodness.

4. *Revealing our delight in another's goodness*—The last step in the movement of affirming love that creates belonging is to let our delight in another's goodness show, especially in nonverbal ways, and to experience that from others. Since 10% of the impact of our communication comes from the

content of our words and the other 90% comes from our nonverbal messages (facial expression, tone of voice, pitch, body posture, etc.). We can lie with our words, but the look in our eyes and the feeling of our muscles when we hug someone don't lie. Simple things convey to us that we are good and that we are loved, such as the way a friend's face lights up when we enter a room, or the warmth in another's arms in a hug. Straightforwardly asking others to care for us in these ways is healthy. Asking for what we need is a healthy way of taking care of ourselves and affirming our right to need other human beings. All of us can help restore in one another the sense of belonging to our true selves by the way we speak to one another, look at one another, and hold one another. That is how my hurts are being healed and my losses restored. Addictive behavior is rooted in shame. Shame originates when the interpersonal bridges that connect us to others are broken and we are left feeling that we do not belong, even to ourselves. Affirmation restores those broken bridges and creates in us a sense of belonging to our real selves, others, God, and the universe.

This little exercise from the Linns' book may help you get in touch with your belonging needs.

Prayer Exercise: getting in touch with how you've been given the gift of affirmation.

Sit comfortably and grow quiet inside.

Recall a moment in your life when you felt nourished and filled by the presence of another person.

Imagine yourself there again, and breathe into yourself once more the gift of belonging to yourself that you received in that moment.

In whatever way you wish, thank that person and God for the gift they gave you, a part of yourself that can never be taken away from you.

So whether we are talking about belonging in a therapeutic community with emotional intimacy defined secularly by Scott Peck, or by Larry Crabb for the Christian community, or about an educational community of which Parker Palmer speaks, or about a spiritual community in the church of which Soo Inn Tan or Jim Kallum speak, we want to create emotional safety for the people with whom we are in loving community. It is a place where you know you belong, of which the Linns speak.

The Importance of Confidentiality in Community

During the Pastor's Sabbath Retreats I led, we attempted to build together just that kind of community, which is emotionally safe and enables participants to be able to retreat and relax together, protecting each other by keeping all confidences and not using "cross talk" or crossing over and talking about someone else's issues instead of our own. At the retreats, we focused on our own issues, reflecting on our lives in silence and solitude, praying that God would give us His perspective on our own selves, on our relationships with others, and on our own ministry.

There are four major tools for this process: utilizing the "Sharing Guidelines" from Mark and Julianne Maki's *Christian Adults in Recovery* materials, telling our stories, giving feedback to each other, and praying for one another. This community building process requires our using the guidelines for sharing when we share with each other in our group. We must learn these guidelines in detail to see that the two main ingredients needed are confidentiality and the no cross talk rule taken from the recovery movement. This is essentially learning to truly actively listen to each other with empathy.

Every good leader is a listener. In the foreword of Max Depree's book *Leadership is an Art (DePree 1989:10-11)*, James O'Toole comments, "The true leader enables followers to realize their full potential!" Leaders must know their own beliefs and have clearly thought them through. Then, leaders will have the "self-confidence . . . to encourage contrary opinions" and "to abandon themselves to the strengths of others." In short, the true leader listens. The leader listens to the ideas, needs, aspirations, and wishes of the followers. Then, within the context of his own or her own well-developed system of beliefs, the leader responds to these in an appropriate manner.

When we listen, we keep our friends safe by keeping their confidences. During group events seeking community, and thereby requiring confidentiality, I always encourage people to use a confidentiality covenant agreement. One example of a confidentiality agreement and Mark and Julianne Maki's "Guidelines for Sharing" are given here.

Confidentiality Covenant

I hereby promise:

To love and respect my brothers and sisters at this retreat by keeping strictly confidential who I see here and everything shared by individuals in this place. I understand that this protection means that I will not pass on personal information that I learn here even with my spouse or any other person unless I have written permission from the people involved. With my signature, I set a seal on my lips!

By signing this covenant, I give the retreat team permission to consult together in their team prayer meetings concerning retreat participants when any one of them are stuck; thus needing advice, support or prayer from the other team members.

We, the team, promise not to take any information out of our team meetings away from this place. With our signatures, we set a seal on our lips.

Signature _____ Date _____

Maki's Guidelines for Sharing

These guidelines for group interaction, taken from Mark and Julianne Maki's book *Christian Adults in Recovery,* will help create an environment of trust, safety and support in our group. The facilitator is not a therapist. The facilitator's job is to maintain these guidelines.

I. Assure Confidentiality

    a. Everything you hear in our meetings should be kept confidential. No member of this group is ever discussed outside of the group--not even with another group member.

    b. Our healing is dependent upon the trust we have in one another, and the freedom we feel to share openly and honestly, without fear of exposure outside of the meetings.

II. Avoid Cross Talk

    a. Cross talk is talking to another person about their issues rather than discussing our own issues. We may refer briefly to what another person has said, but each of us needs to talk about our own experiences, feelings or problems.

    b. We must be especially careful to avoid cross talk which involves criticism, advice, denial of another person's pain, or questioning.

        i. Criticism: If we feel criticized or judged, our response will be to stop sharing and we will experience increased guilt, hopelessness and isolation. We need to be free to admit to certain personal negative things, knowing that the response of the group will be loving acceptance. (The only exception to the "no criticism" rule is when a member says or does something that violates the guidelines of this group. Such behavior is subject to discussion and group decision.)

ii. Advice: We tend to resist advice often because it leaves us feeling "talked down to." Sometimes we feel the advice is given without understanding or sympathy for the particulars of our personality, our history and our situation. Even when we know the advice to be good, we may feel powerless to follow it. As a result, even good advice may leave us feeling hopeless. It is advice when we share our experience motivated by a desire to fix or guide someone in the group. We are able to learn and grow from receiving love, support and acceptance and from seeing others getting well. What we share here is not advice, but our own experience, strength and hope. If you would like some feedback or advice, ask for it to be given after the end of the meeting.

iii. Denial of Painful Emotions: It is very important that each member of our group feel free to express painful emotions such as shame, grief or anger, without being judged.

iv. Questioning: Questions for more information or clarification can be intrusive or meant to fix the person who is sharing causing them to feel shamed and result in their shutting down. We can ask for something to be repeated if we were unable to hear.

III. Please share only about yourself.

a. In your sharing use "I" statements.

b. Don't disclose for or give criticism of your spouse or anyone else.

c. Don't tell stories about others.

d. Don't preach about what we should think, feel or be.

e. Wait for the person speaking to finish before you speak.

f. It is okay to remain silent.

g. Our sharing time is not intended to put anyone on the spot or require anyone to talk or disclose more than they are comfortable sharing.

IV. Stick to the original sharing question.

   V. Please don't touch anyone in the group without
      asking permission.

      a. Sometimes reaching over to touch someone
         who is crying or in pain can feel intrusive by
         the person being touched. Feelings are often
         shut down when we are touched unexpectedly,
         even if it was meant as a caring gesture.

      b. We can ask for appropriate touch if we want it
         ("Would someone be willing to hold my hand
         as I talk about this?" or, "Could I give you a
         hug?"). We also need to be free to say "No"
         when we do not want touch, even if someone
         asks.

As I go through the guidelines for sharing above, I
seek to explain how to give positive feedback or speak the
love language of grace to a person and then how to pray for
them. I think that the language of law is our mother tongue
and the language of grace is our second language.
Sometimes, as with learning a second language (like German
was for me) we feel awkward speaking it, and under
pressure we often revert back to the mother tongue. We
must fight this tendency and learn fluency in the new
language, the language of grace. The feedback we offer to
the person who has shared their story is to be positive,
accepting, affirmative, uplifting, and encouraging words
only. Notice that I did not say the three naughty C's—
criticizing, complaining, or condemning—which is our
mother tongue, the language of law. Sometimes we don't

recognize other shades of this because it so prevalent in our speech.

After a person share's their story, it is time for gentle and loving feedback from the hearers. During the time of feedback, it is not appropriate to correct the story-tellers (by saying "You should realize . . . " or "You could do this better by . . . "), to direct them (by saying "You ought to . . . "), or to offer prophetic words ("God is going to change you or this situation by . . . "). Any corrections, directions, advice giving, or prophecy is defined as "cross talk" and explained above in Maki's "Guidelines for Sharing." Instead, after each person shares their story, we are simply to receive that person and their story like a gift. Like a precious treasured gift, we hold them and their story in our minds and hearts and notice their goodness for several quiet minutes. Having heard their story, we will take turns offering them feedback, reflecting back to the person the goodness, strengths, beauty, outstanding traits, gifts, and godly characteristics that we see in them. These positive reflections will be recorded on a piece of paper and given to the person later to reread and keep to read again on a rainy day.

I have often participated in this process of sharing and giving feedback, and it has been a source of joy and strength for me.

My Story in the Light of His Story

From the cradle to the grave God is forming His purpose in us. At a personal growth seminar in the spring of 1996, I was helped to write out my "Life Purpose," in which purpose is where I am aiming not where I have arrived. This represents areas in which God is working on me presently and has been doing healing in my heart in the past. This is the life purpose I wrote for myself in 1996 and modified in 2002:

> *I am a carefree, feminine, and wise woman of God, joyously singing and dancing as I tenaciously and passionately bring healing with compassion, in a context of loving community with grace and truth and accountability, to souls in His Kingdom.*

Just before I left Austria for Houston in 2002, I added to my life purpose the phrase "in a context of loving community with grace and truth and accountability." It was because God was showing me new things that He wanted me to live out since the time I had originally written my life purpose in 1996. I also took the time to write out my story so that I could share it with others in the context of confidential community. As I relate my story, you may see how God has been forming this purpose in me along the way. See if you can sight His handiwork.

> On the inside, I am a struggling, scared little girl with a broken, lonely heart who is often very angry at those who hurt me. Jesus has been healing me and teaching me how to bring healing to others by listening to me first, accepting me, loving me, and then telling me, "Go and do likewise!"

On the outside, I am a returning missionary, pastor, and counselor after our second 6-year term in Europe. I came back to North America from Innsbruck, Austria, after waving our goods off in a container on the 19th of June, 2002, for Houston, Texas. I came back for a home assignment literally because I was born in Houston, Texas, in 1944 (making me 70), and I returned after being away, (counting my college years which were spent at Wheaton College in Illinois) almost 40 years. I experienced "reverse culture shock" big time! Houston had changed; but so had I. It did not feel like home anymore.

I have been married to Peter Davids for 48 years and we have three adult Christian children. Our elder daughter lives in Calgary, Alberta, with her husband and three daughters, aged 18 and 16 and 13 years. Our middle daughter helped out for four years with her husband in the Croydon Vineyard south of London, England, as interns and both had secular jobs on the side. They now have a twelve-year-old boy named Nathaniel, a nine-year-old Benjamin, a six-year-old Joseph, and a three-year-old boy named Ian who was born on June 25th, 2012. They moved back to Canada where Brent's parents live in Regina, Sask., in the summer of 2004. Through a series of tragic events, including Brent's falling off a ladder, breaking his neck, injuring his back, and then contracting meningitis, and their house's burning down and their having rebuilt it, they landed in St. Stephen where Brent was attending the university and dividing our house on Union Street into two apartments. Brent has since graduated from St. Stephen's University and helped to build a business. Our son graduated with a degree in computer science from Simon Fraser University in Vancouver, BC, in June of 2003 and married a lovely Christian woman in January 2003. They live in BC where he works in programming computer games. His wife enjoys cake decorating, and they have a daughter, Adana, who is four years old and Eli who is one year old.. All three of our children were living lives honoring to God, they married three Christian Canadians, and they are all active in the church. Wow! God is full of grace! This fact released us to go to the mission field in 1996.

My four grandparents were all economically poor Texans. My paternal grandparents lived in Lott, Texas, near Waco and picked cotton as children and young adults. My maternal grandparents lived in the Livingston area in east Texas and had a filling station and a small repair business and green grocer in Columbus, Texas, while my mom was growing up. My Christian maternal grandmother made a garden for 90 years out of her 98 years on this earth. She planted potatoes when she was four in her father's garden and made her own last vegetable garden when she was 94. I'm the avid gardener in our family, having spent some delightful summers with this grandma when I was growing up.

My father was born in Lott, Texas, and his family moved to Houston when he was seven. He became a Christian when he was 14. He had one year at the University of Houston and then worked as a plasterer. Later he became a chemical operator at Rohm and Haas Chemical Co. located on the Houston ship channel. My mom, who did one year in a business college and worked as a secretary before marriage, was a housewife until I was in the fifth grade when she got a job with Petro-Tex Chemical Co. on the Houston ship channel working as an executive secretary for one of the vice presidents. She enjoyed working with her hands in craftwork, sewing, painting, and ceramics.

I was born during World War II on October 18, 1944 in Houston, Texas, to Christian parents in St. Joseph's hospital and came home to my paternal grandparents' house where my mom was living because my dad, a US marine, had been shipped out to the South Pacific on the island of Okinawa. He did not see me until I was 13 months old after the war was over. My dad had a rough time getting to know his little daughter because I was deathly afraid of him and would not let him hold me when he returned. It took almost a year for me to be completely at peace with him. He won my heart by blowing bubbles for hours at the seaside. Those memories may be part of the reason I love the ocean and honeymooned in Galveston.

At age twenty-one months, on the day my brother was born, nine months after my father returned from the war, I became angry at being displaced from my prime position in the world. I had represented hope and happiness to my parents and grandparents during the war. I was at the center of their world and had enjoyed their attention. The emotion of anger has dominated my life and I did not even become aware of it until I was 40 when I had teenagers of my own and walked into a Vineyard conference with a migraine headache, but that is another story. My sister was born when I was four years old, and she has become one of my dearest friends on earth. We were sibling rivals until I returned after my first year of college when we became friends. We did not live with or near each other until I returned to Houston 40 years later in 2002. While I lived in Canada, we talked by phone for an hour on Friday mornings.

At age seven, as I began first grade, I contracted polio. I remember a night when I tried to get up and go to the bathroom but could not walk without excruciating pain. My father came running at my screams and picked me up and carried me. I was hospitalized and diagnosed with a light case of polio, which had paralyzed my left leg and my stomach muscles. With rest and therapy I could walk again within several months and could return to school. During my stay in the hospital, I met Lana Lary who was my age and who had a severe case of polio, paralyzing both her legs. She lived only a few blocks from me, and I pushed her to school in her wheel chair for several years until her arms were strong enough to push herself.

At age nine, I made a public confession of faith in Jesus in Monday afternoon Bible school after learning the verse Romans 7:18, which convicted me of my sin: "I know that good itself does not dwell in me, that is, in my sinful nature. For I have the desire to do what is good, but I cannot carry it out."

At age ten, my father commented to me that he saw me as a peacemaker because he noticed that I was not happy if any of my friends were having relational problems. I worked mediating between them until there was peace between all.

At age 11, I was baptized and took my first communion. It was about this time that I went into

Granny Green's Sunday school class, and Granny taught me to pray. I remember well the summer that I took Barbara, my friend from school, to camp, and Granny and I used to come back to our cabin and pray for her to become a Christian. Before the end of camp, Barbara became a Christian, and Granny assured me that it was because of our prayers. I met my dear friend Carolen that year and she is still my friend 59 years later. She lives in Whitney, Texas, with her family.

At age 12, I went to camp and knelt in the woods in Cedar Hill, Texas, and promised God that I would be His missionary. I would go anywhere and do anything that He asked me to do. I never dreamed that it was to be a missionary in German-speaking Europe, to help found a counseling center in Regina, Saskatchewan, to counsel missionaries in the Ivory Coast, to teach the Skilled Helper in Russia with a Ukrainian translator in four house churches, to create Pastors' Sabbath Retreats and direct them for American, Canadian, and Hong Kong pastors, to endure New Brunswick winters as a Professor, to come back to Houston summers and write a book, or to have many of my other adventures, for that matter.

At age 19, I heard God tell me that I needed to "trust God in the dark." My family was on their way to Wheaton, Illinois, to take me to college when we were in a three-car accident. We were all injured. I stayed out of college until January of the next year when I returned on the train with my father. I was walking with a cane, having a metal pin in my broken left femur and having cracked my pelvis and crushed a vertebra in my lower back. My father was walking with crutches, having broken both bones in his right leg below the knee. This was the second time that my left leg kept me from beginning school when it was time to begin. As a result of this accident, I met Peter Davids at Wheaton in summer school. I tried to make up the time that I had missed, and he was trying to go through in three years because he was headed towards a Ph. D. I also developed a phobia of cars as a result of that accident and am still trying to conquer it today. Driving on the freeways in Houston has been helping me a lot to overcome this old problem in my life.

At age 31, I was filled anew with the Holy Spirit, healed, and then prophesied over by my prayer partner, a student, and the academic dean's wife at Missionshaus Bibelschule Wiedenest where Peter and I were teaching in Germany. He was teaching full time in German, and I was teaching two courses in English and doing my first counseling in German in the women's dormitory. We had two little girls by then, aged four and one. Peter had finished his Ph. D. the year before in England. Our first daughter was born in Chicago as Peter was studying for his Masters of Divinity Degree, and our second daughter was born during his Ph. D. studies in England. As we left Germany, Peter and I were called forward and were prayed over. I was blessed to go and begin a counseling ministry in the US, bringing much healing to many.

At age 34, I prayed a prayer that the Spirit of the Living God would breathe on me, mold me, and make me. I had started a prayer group consisting of six women who were faculty wives and women students in Trinity School for Ministry where Peter was teaching New Testament in Sewickley, PA. Six weeks later, Elizabeth Jane, our third daughter was born. Six weeks after that, she died from Crib Death or SIDS. God woke me in the night with a ten-part open-eye vision after she died, which began to help me understand how Peter and I were entering into the Father's pain when His son died on the cross. The spiritual "Mary, don't you weep, baby Jesus is gonna die" was going over and over in my mind between the sections of this open-eye vision, which brought great hope to me. I was at a Plymouth Brethren's Women's Missionary Conference when I heard the Lord speak to me as I listened to a missionary nurse. She shared the story of her work in the Philippines with a six-week-old baby girl who was healed from malaria as she and her husband prayed for her. I heard God say to me that with that baby girl's life, He had chosen life to bring Him glory; but with Elizabeth, He had chosen death. He told me that He was sovereign in my life. I cried and cried and cried. My Plymouth Brethren lady friends did not know what to do with me and with my wailing that day. After a miscarriage six months later, I became pregnant with our son, Ian. I got a letter from Granny Green, my Sunday school teacher, in March of that year saying that she hoped that I had a boy because boys are more fun. (She had raised four boys mostly by herself, having been widowed at age 35.) Granny died in April at the age of 90, and Ian was born in May and brought an incredible amount of joy into our lives and into the lives of his two sisters.

At age 40, I remember standing in the women's washroom and saying to God, "You and I know that You have called me to minister in this church whether the elders lay hands on me or not!" There was a laying-on-of-hands ceremony that morning as the elders prayed for Peter as he would take a position of preaching elder in that church. I went on to set up my first counseling ministry in that Plymouth Brethren church, training six other lay counselors.

As I have mentioned previously, at age 46, I burned out. I was trying to deal with adjustment to a new province in Canada, tension in my marriage, a rebellious 16-year old daughter, a full-time counseling practice in our home, my volunteering in our church on a tambourine team, helping my husband mentor a group of his seminary students on Tuesday nights, leading a small group, listening to a video series by John Wimber on Healing on Thursday nights, and initiating a Friday committee meeting in my home that spearheaded a Christian counseling center in Regina, Saskatchewan, called The Caring Place. I had to get some counseling to see what was wrong: "severe burnout" was the diagnosis. I had to take one year off from everything except being a wife and a mother and the duties that came along with those responsibilities. I was overwhelmed with feelings of hopelessness, helplessness, and despair. A Catholic nun gave me spiritual direction for that year and had me take a spiritual retreat at a nearby monastery after three months. She stopped me from doing my regular Bible reading each day of a psalm, an Old Testament chapter, and a New Testament chapter. In its place, she had me meditate for three whole months on one verse—Psalm 46:10—"Be still and know that I am God." When I went to the monastery for my retreat, the verse was hanging behind the altar in one-foot high green letters. I learned that the verse had been there for three months and would be taken down soon. I was undone at how God had intimately spoken into my life. That year of crisis caused a huge spiritual growth spurt in me. I learned that I needed a Sabbath rhythm in my life. I needed to do regular spiritual retreats with a spiritual director. The spiritual disciplines needed to be part of my lifestyle. I needed to slow down and smell the flowers. Scared to death that I had forgotten how, I began counseling again 17 months after I had laid it down. God is good, for not only did He heal my burnout, but He also taught me many things and set me on a new and deeper path with Him.

At age 52, in December of 1998, our contract was not renewed at Schloss Mittersill in Austria. Peter and I moved to Innsbruck and began working with the German-speaking Vineyards. I was angry at our boss and at God for removing us from our position in the castle. I could not understand why that would have happened when my ministry was blossoming and I was growing so much personally with teaching in several countries in Eastern Europe and in Russia. People were coming for counseling from all over Europe and I just could not understand it! I felt hurt, rejected and betrayed. My father died that next year, and I had to have two lumps removed from my breast, which were hard experiences to go through in a foreign country using a foreign language. I felt as if I were in the desert as we moved to Innsbruck because I was on the shelf as far as ministry was concerned, and I was really struggling to understand Austrian German. I felt like a little child starting all over in a new culture. I was very lonely and I missed my dad. There was a prophecy spoken over me in Switzerland at a Vineyard pastor's conference. The man, who did not know me or my situation, saw me in a field looking very lost because the Lord had taken my sickle away and I could not do my harvesting job anymore. Then he told me to look up, for there came the Lord driving up in a combine machine, and He invited me to climb up with Him and begin harvesting fields, not just one field.

At age 58, the Lord called Peter and me to Houston, Texas, out of our job with the German-speaking Vineyards. But before I left Innsbruck, the Lord birthed in me the vision of "bringing community everywhere I go" as I read Larry Crabb's and Scott Peck's books on this topic. I went to Houston, and the first thing I was asked to do was to take over their Community Care Ministry from an assistant pastor in the Sugar Land Vineyard. So I set about to build community first and then to build a ministry. I also built a ministry called Pastors' Sabbath Retreats for the American Vineyards, ministering to burned-out pastors. This was all done in the context of community.

At age 62, I found myself in St. Stephen's University in St. Stephen, New Brunswick, lecturing in the psychology department, doing some counseling, initiating Pastors' Sabbath Retreats in Canada, living in the same house with our middle daughter and her family. For me this was a positive adventure in family relationships and learning to lecture in a university. However, this Texan gal froze in the cold winters of New Brunswick.

My hobbies are playing the piano, quilting, tatting, gardening, and reading. I began two "friendship triads" with four other friends to proactively work on forming friendships in our new place. I also lead a mentoring group of six university students. I led a recovery group for women in our church and directed the faculty quiet day one year.

At age 66, I left SSU with my husband, who had taken a voluntary unpaid sabbatical, and lived in Houston, Texas, with my sister and her husband for the winter and spring, and I began writing this book again. My husband taught at Houston Baptist University and Houston Graduate School of Theology as an adjunct professor, and he also spent time writing books. I spent March in Vancouver helping my daughter-in-law with her first baby. In April of 2011, my husband, Peter, got a permanent job at Houston Baptist University, so we made a trip back to St. Stephen for our son-in-law's graduation from St. Stephen's University with an honors degree in history. Then we resigned our position there. Next came the arduous task of packing up our belongings and moving to Houston a second time and finding a place to live there.

At age 70, I find that God is still at work forming His purpose in me because I am not finished yet. He used my losses of polio, the car wreck, Elizabeth's death, leaving Austin Ave. Chapel where we were pastoring, my burn-out experience in Regina, our leaving Schloss Mittersill in Austria, the death of my parents, and the loss of my job with the American and Canadian Vineyards to form His purpose in me. The desert experiences of the wreck, burnout, and leaving the Schloss were designed especially to form me into His image. He has formed a listening ear and a healing presence in a compassionate and wise person, giving me the cause of forming community, bringing peace and a safe place wherever I go. He has also made me into a trail blazer for women in ministry and one to bring healing to tired, worn out, and wounded pastors and missionaries. My hat is off to a God who cares enough about me to refine me in these ways and allow me to partner with Him in his kingdom work on earth. He is indeed good and gracious to me! Praise His holy name! I'm presently looking for His kingdom work, which has my name written on it, in Houston, Texas. But in the meantime, I've been writing on my book.

The latest crisis is my husband's two seizures resulting in me driving him for 6 months. This gave me one more chance to learn to surrender.

I chose to go to His church and have become a daughter of the King. I gave a spring retreat for them, trained a new group of daughters and spoke at a Diocesan Assembly. Working in the food pantry, helping out with the Kairos prison ministry, and helping with the Family Promise Ministry has been fun in our new church in Houston.

Feedback

Remember, a vital part of building community is not only sharing your story, but also receiving loving feedback from the hearers. As I have shared this testimony many times, I have also had the opportunity to receive feedback from others. Here is some feedback that I've received from different groups who have heard my story. These examples are positive, encouraging, uplifting, affirming, and accepting, and are excellent examples of good feedback.

In August 2004 at the first PSR Retreat, I was given a new name by a fellow pastor: "The Tiny Towering Tender Tenacious Trailblazer." This new name encouraged me greatly.

In October 2004, on my 60th Birthday, a team member named Lisa Merchant, whom I had trained for the church ministry that I was then leading, presented this poem to me:

"Instrument of Renewal"

*You were the instrument used
to cut through our sleeping minds,
to awaken a buried knowing
and bring it into the Light.*

*The precision of your awesome task,
has pierced our gentle hearts
exposing the many jigsaw pieces
that no longer fit this life.*

*The smoothness of your blade of truth
sank, into depth unknown.
The veins of fears were severed
and new ideas emerged.*

*The sharpness of your probing edge
caused us moments of stress and pain,
then quickly produced within us
an unshakeable belief.*

*The steadiness of your solid steel
gave us the faith and strength
to explore our own path
as instruments in this world.*

Rest easy, instrument of renewal,
your aim has hit its mark.
Now others will see the message
you've left within us
as we go forth.

Lisa also wrote the following second poem and presented it to me as I was leaving Houston in June 2006.

"A Light"

A light sent to us to bring us warmth
and invite us into a welcoming presence,
A light sent to awaken in us a belonging
buried within our neglected brokenness,
A light sent to illuminate our hidden gifts
and longing to share ourselves
with this wounded broken world,
A light sent to give strength to us as wounded
healers
so we could be a light to others,
Now, a community of light, united in love,
fueled by this passion sent by God above.

In April 2007, a student group gave me the following feedback:

You've had a caring heart from your youth.
You've had a life of Christian service.
You have a tenacious faith.
You are one who has overcome.
You listen to God. You've had positive responses
to unhappy milestones in life.
You have a positive self-image.
You are an example of determination,
perseverance, and growth.
You have an ability to adapt.

You are comfortable telling stories about yourself.
You are able to forgive.
You have personal and spiritual disciplines in place in your life.

During the fall of 2007, I received this feedback from a different student group.

Your leap of faith challenges me in my own walk of faith.
Your family and this move fit into God's big picture.
One can see the Father's heart in you.
I'm impressed with your story of you as a young girl who had a mission to bring people into community, and then to see how you fed and nurtured these gifts in yourself.
Your life has been an expression of the missing link in my mentoring.
Your passion is such an encouragement to others.
Grace is demonstrated in you—in your talk, prayers, and your walk of faith.
Your skills of attentive listening are also evident in how you listen to God's voice.
Your honesty and truth in looking at yourself and your life are admirable.
I'm amazed at someone who truly knows who they are.
Your presence is a gift to all that know you.
God's healing presence shines through you.
I've enjoyed watching how your story has expressed God's transformation in you each time that I've heard it.

September 2009 feedback from a student group:

Judy, a Woman of Faith
Your story makes me feel hopeful.
Your story is humbling. It makes me realize
that you are a very human teacher.
You are strong, intelligent, open, and honest.
You have strength in weakness.
You are full of grace and strength.

February 2010 feedback from a student group:

You are strong, steadfast, and courageous.
You are caring.
You are obedient.
You have faith.
You have respect for others.

I have become a real fan of this story time. I actually began this practice in recovery groups for sexually abused women and saw so much healing come from this experience that I then decided to use it in retreats for pastors and for university professors, in student mentoring groups, as well as in many other recovery groups. Telling your personal story is a very healing experience.

An example of just how healing during a recovery group in which someone refused to tell her story. I excused her from it, but she then dropped out of the group. A month went by, and with two weeks left in our three-month recovery group process, I got a phone call one evening from this woman begging me to allow her to come back to the group so that she could tell her story. She had not been able to sleep, thinking that she was missing out on this important, life-giving, and healing experience and opportunity. She returned to the group and told her story the next week, and it was one of the most healing experiences that she had ever had in her entire life. The story of her sexual abuse had been a deep, dark, hidden, and reluctantly-told secret, which had completely poisoned her life; but the relief and peace plus the positive feedback and support of the group were amazingly healing for this person, in spite of the great reluctance she had to overcome to just get the story out in the open. She thanked the group, God, and me for the opportunity after she was done. Getting to the actual telling was a real mountain of shame and guilt to climb, and a whole other story in itself. But it was a victorious and happy mountain for her in the end, which brought amazing healing to her.

Of course, this is a dramatic story with a happy ending, but many who come to tell their stories have milder but similar feelings to overcome before they can tell their story. It seems to always be worth the effort though. I would encourage you to write and tell your story to a supportive group if you have never done so before. The personal growth coming from such an experience might surprise you greatly.

To build community, I teach people two rules from the recovery movement: confidentiality and no cross talk. I also encourage the utilization of the two tools of story telling and feedback.

Telling Your Story

There are so many benefits of telling your story, although it can be hard to identify them when you're feeling scared, guilty, or ashamed about doing so. Listed below are some common reasons why people find it empowering to tell their story.

Check off the ones that might apply to you:

☐ Telling my story will help me overcome feelings of shame about my life.

☐ I'll find out that I'm no longer alone or different—others have suffered too.

☐ I'll experience someone else's compassion and love.

☐ I'll expose the past and present dysfunctional aspects of my life.

☐ I'll stop following dysfunctional rules.

☐ Once I tell, I can get help and support.

☐ I'll move through my denial.

☐ I'll get in touch with my feelings.

☐ When I'm more honest, my relationships will become more intimate.

☐ People around me will get information and be less confused about what I'm going through.

☐ I'll establish myself as a person in the present dealing with the dysfunctional issues I have experienced as a child that continue to influence my life.

☐ I'll help end the cycle of dysfunction by breaking the silence in which it thrives.

☐ I'll be a model for others who are dealing with similar issues.

☐ Telling will empower me to walk through the process of healing.

☐ I'll expose hidden fears and possibly hidden strengths.

☐ I'll feel relieved and receive peace.

☐ Telling will help me recall the facts so that I can reflect accurately on my life.

☐ I'll retrace the path of the pain so the wounds can be healed.

☐ Telling helps to ground me in truth so that I can begin to deal with the past and   present.

☐ Telling my story makes me more aware of my need for God who is my Helper and Healer.

Because you have only thirty minutes to tell your story, I suggest streamlining it by writing notes on note cards or scripting the entire story. One way to think through your story is to find significant milestones in each decade of your life, perhaps places where God spoke to you or where

you grew significantly. As you formulate your story do the
following:

1. Describe your story factually and objectively, like
   a newspaper reporter would.
2. Recall the facts of those significant milestones in
   your life. (You will want to include the following:
   how old you were, the date, time and place, which
   significant persons were there, what the situation
   was, what special events took place, etc.). Work
   by decades of your life.
3. As you walk through your story, access,
   remember and share the feelings from each
   situation.
4. Reflect on how the incidents affect you now, on
   how you see them differently, and express this.
   See how you have matured and have found
   meaning and purpose in this painful part of your
   life.

In the process of recalling your life story, there are
two steps, which you need to take. First you must remember
the story. Then you must recognize your pain and the need
for healing and finding meaning in it.

To remember history can be a great blessing or a
great curse. Today's Jews certainly call it both. When
referring to the Nazi Holocaust, they darkly but sincerely
chant, "Never forget!" To forget invites repetition. However,
remembering this tragedy in their history bathes the Jew

with bitter images and devastating pain, both of which can erode the spirit and scar the psyche yet again.

We want to take George Santayana's famous phrase to heart: "Those who forget the past are doomed to repeat it." G.K. Chesterton's observation applies as well: "We are destined to misunderstand the story we find ourselves in." So we want to remember our stories to discern their meaning and purpose.

Alternatively, you may be thinking just the opposite: I can't get it out of my mind. I don't want to keep dwelling on what happened, especially if it includes painful events. We don't want you to dwell on what happened either; instead, we want you to talk about it to a trusted person and get it out in the open. In doing so, the experience moves from being pictures in your mind to pictures with a story. Ironically, this kind of remembering is empowering. It's the type of personal recollection that has a corrective nature all its own.

As you remember and formulate your story, do the following:

1. *Recall the facts.* Describe, in play-by-play fashion, specific painful events. If you're angry because your father "let you down," describe the specific events that typified what he did. How old were you? Where were you? What was the situation? Who was there? How did the situation unfold? What exactly did he do that hurt you? What resulted from the hurt? How long ago did this

event occur? How did the situation end? Describe it factually, much like a newspaper reporter would.

2. *Retrace the path of the pain.* By describing the facts, the past comes alive in the present. Of course, it's always been alive—covered up, but alive. How so? Your past hasn't really passed if you still carry its pain. As you describe the wound, this confrontation may become tangled with emotion and discussed in the present tense, as if the situation were ongoing; you may tell the story with flushed face, raised voice, and exaggerated behavior. But once the painful events are released into words, it's possible to heal the soul wound. The wounded self is no longer cloaked in denial.

3. *Now complete the story.* Access and remember the feelings that burst to the surface during the episode. Were you angry? If so, what about? Were you afraid? How afraid? Terrified, maybe? What did you think was actually going on? What did it mean to you? What did you want to happen that didn't? How did you respond? How did you want to respond? How did you feel as you responded? How did others respond? How did this incident affect you? How does the incident affect you now? How do you feel, right now, as you relive the event?

Answer these questions and your whole story begins to emerge. And as you translate your life experience into a story, you externalize it, you place it in the open air so those who are helping you heal can better understand you and what brought you there. Using words to describe what happened to you also helps you gain control of the event. Once it's told as a story, the thing that happened to you has a beginning and an end and words with finite meanings describing it. It's no longer some unrestrained, giant, all-consuming, never-ceasing turmoil you could never hope to deal with in a million years. It's now bounded by meaningful words, and you can now begin to deal with it.

The goal for a healing participant or a helper during this process is quite simple: help facilitate the story and encourage it along when the person is hesitant or fearful.

After you've taken the time to remember the story, make sure you engage in the second step of recognizing your pain and the need for healing. Professional counselors often say, "You can't treat what you don't see." These first two steps, remember your story and recognize your pain, have been defined to help heighten your awareness of the pain that plagues your soul. But why experience that pain all over again? I think you'll see why this step is necessary as I guide you through this part of the process:

1. *See purpose in the pain.* Pain has a purpose. In fact, the pain we feel as we talk about our story has several important ones. In taming an emotional storm, the act of accepting primary

pain is validating. Up to this point, your emotional life may have been shrouded in guilt and shame as the result of believing yourself wrong for feeling as you did. Giving yourself permission to feel primary pain tells you that you were right to feel as you did. You may need to forgive yourself or the person who hurt you. Your story now has meaning as you get in touch with the purpose for your pain.

2. *In addition, when we acknowledge our pain and vulnerability, we become more aware of our need for God.* Jesus said, "Come to me, all you who are weary and burdened, and I will give you rest (Matthew 11:28). To come to Him with our burden first requires us to acknowledge that we have one and that we're weary and anguished from carrying it. And as we lay it at the cross, we quickly find He's our soul's great comforter, our refuge from life's storms—even our emotional storms. In II Corinthians 12:8-10, Paul described his struggle with personal weakness, weakness he saw with divine purpose. God told him, "My grace is sufficient for you."

Telling your personal story has many benefits, and healing usually results from the process. Not only have I seen tremendous effects from the use of these tools, but Scripture also speaks to the benefits of telling your story. Revelation 12: 1-12 talks about defeating our enemy with the word of our testimony or our story! This story-telling thing may be far more important than we know. Our God has written His story of grace down in the Bible to tell us about Himself and His plans:

> *A great portent appeared in heaven: a woman clothed with the sun, with the moon under her feet, and on her head a crown of twelve stars. She was pregnant and was crying out in birth pangs, in the agony of giving birth. Then another portent appeared in heaven: a great red dragon, with seven heads and ten horns, and seven diadems on his heads.*
>
> *His tail swept down a third of the stars of heaven and threw them to the earth. Then the dragon stood before the woman who was about to bear a child, so that he might devour her child as soon as it was born. And she gave birth to a son, a male child, who is to rule all the nations with a rod of iron. But her child was snatched away and taken to God and to his throne; 6 and the woman fled into the wilderness, where she has a place prepared by God, so that there she can be nourished for one thousand two hundred sixty days.*
>
> *And war broke out in heaven; Michael and his angels fought against the dragon. The dragon and his angels fought back, but they were defeated, and there was no longer any place for them in heaven.*
>
> *The great dragon was thrown down, that ancient serpent, who is called the Devil and Satan, the deceiver of the whole world—he was*

thrown down to the earth, and his angels were thrown down with him.

Then I heard a loud voice in heaven, proclaiming,

"Now have come the salvation and the power and the kingdom of our God and the authority of his Messiah, for the accuser of our comrades has been thrown down, who accuses them day and night before our God.

But they have conquered him by the blood of the Lamb and by the word of their testimony, for they did not cling to life even in the face of death.

Rejoice then, you heavens and those who dwell in them!

But woe to the earth and the sea, for the devil has come down to you with great wrath, because he knows that his time is short!" (NRSV)

Did you hear what I heard in that passage? Telling our story in the light of "The Story," or God's grace story, will defeat the enemy of our souls, the accuser of the comrades. (The King James Version says "the accuser of the brethren," meaning the brothers and sisters in the family of God.) Brethren, let us tell our stories because this is the way we can bring the kingdom of God on earth and defeat the enemy. Also the entire mystery of the Incarnation is tied up in this telling of our story, because John1:1 says Jesus was the Word. The Holy Son of God is the Word, and He became flesh. We put our life into words when we tell our story. The vague ideas running around in our heads become concrete or become incarnate when we put them into words. We bring our story out into the open or into the light when we tell it: thus our life has eternal meaning.

We see that story telling is a powerful tool accompanied by the two rules from the recovery movement of confidentiality and no cross talk. And as I said above the tool of story telling will help build community if used with feedback that is spoken in the language of grace coupled with prayer for a person. So to live your life wisely in a balanced manner in order to make it to the finish line doing well, you must value and incorporate into your life the support of a faithful community. That community will be God's hands on this earth to help you get back up if you stumble, fall, become ill, or need time to convalesce. The practice of the grace of community in conjunction with a healthy Sabbath rhythm allows you to live a meaningful life that counts for eternity thus empowered to pause, pray, and play.

Bibliography

Below are some suggested additional resources from which I have gleaned much regarding the rhythms of pause, pray, and play.

Anderson, Fil. *Running On Empty*. Waterbrook, 2004.

Baldwin, Christina. *One to One*. M. Evans and Co., 1991.

Benner, David. *Surrender to Love*. IVP, 2003.

Benner, David. The Gift of Being Yourself. IVP, 2004.

Bonhoeffer, Deitrich. *Life Together*. Harper San Francisco, 1954.

Boudreaux, Keith. *Getting to the Root*. Legacy Press, 1999.

Brandt, Leslie. *Psalms Now*. Concordia Publishing House, 1974.

Casey, Michael. *Sacred Reading*. Ligouri, 1995.

Champlin, Joseph M. *Slow Down*. Sorin Books, 2004.

Chittister, Joan D. *Gateway to Resurrection*. Benetvision, 1999.

Chittester, Joan D. *Illuminated Life*. Orbis Books, 2000.

Crabb, Larry. *Connecting*. Word Publishing, 1997.

Crabb, Larry. *Shattered Dreams*. Waterbrook Press, 2001.

Crabb, Larry. *Soul Talk*. Integrity Publishers, 2003.

Crabb, Larry.*The Pressures Off*. Waterbrook Press, 2002.

Crabb, Larry. *The Pressure's Off Workbook*. Waterbrook Press, 2002.

Crabb, Larry. *The Safest Place on Earth*. Word Publishing, 1999.

Dawn Marva. J. *A Royal "Waste" of Time*. Eerdmans, 1999.

Demarest, Bruce. *Soul Guide*. Navpress, 2003.

Demarest, Bruce. *Satisfy Your Soul.* Navpress, 1999.

Eldredge, John. *The Journey of Desire.* Thomas Nelson, 1993.

Eldredge, John. *The Sacred Romance*. Thomas Nelson, 1997.

Eldredge, John. *Wild at Heart*. Thomas Nelson, 2001.

Eldredge, John. *Waking the Dead*. Thomas Nelson, 2006.

Foster, Richard. *Celebration of Discipline*. Harper & Row, 1978.

Foster, Richard. *Prayer: Finding the Heart's True Home.* Harper San Francisco, 1992.

Foster, Richard. *Streams of Living Water*. Harper San Francisco, 1982.

Gaultiere, William. *A Walk with Your Shepherd & CD*. Moody, 1992.

Hall, Thelma. *Too Deep for Words*. Paulist Press, 1988.

Hansel, Tim. *You Gotta Keep Dancin'.* David C. Cook, 1985.

Heliwig, Monica K. *Guests of God*. Paulist Press, 1999.

Karvan, John. *Peace of Heart*. Harold Press, 1995.

Keen, Sam, and Fox, Anne Valley. *Telling Your Story*. Signet Books, 1974.

Klug, Ronald. *How to Keep a Spiritual Journal*. Thomas Nelson, 1993.

Linn, Dennis, Sheila, Matthew. *Healing the Purpose of Your Life*. Paulist Press, 1999.

Longman, Tremper. *How the Read the Psalms*. IVP, 1988.

McGinn, Bernard. *Early Christian Mystics.* Crossroad Publishers, 2003.

Miley, Jeanie. *Ancient Psalms for Contemporary Pilgrims.* Smyth Helwys Publishers, 2003.

Miller, Donald. *Blue Like Jazz.* Nelson, 2003.

Muller, Wayne. *Sabbath.* Bantum Paperback, 2000.

Norris, Gunilla. *Inviting Silence.* Blue Bridge, 2004.

Nouwen, Henri J.M. *The Heart of Henri Nouwen.* Crossroad Publishers, 2003.

Nouwen, Henri J.M. *Bread for the Journey.* Dartman, Logan, Todd, 1997.

Nouwen, Henri J.M. *Heart Speaks to Heart.* Ave Maria Press, 1989.

Nouwen, Henri J.M. *Here and Now.* Crossroad Publishers, 2002.

Nouwen, Henri J.M. *In the House of the Lord.* Dartman, Logan, Todd, 1986.

Nouwen, Henri J.M. *In the Name of Jesus.* Crossroad Publishers, 1989.

Nouwen, Henri J.M. *The Genesee Diary.* Doubleday and Company, 1976.

Nouwen, Henri J.M. *The Inner Voice of Love.* Random House, 2010.

Nouwen, Henri J.M. *Life of the Beloved.* Dartman, Logan, Todd, 1976.

Nouwen, Henri J. M. *The Inner Voice of Love.* Doubleday, 1996.

Nouwen, Henri J. M. *Life of the Beloved*. London: Hodder and Stoughton, 1992.

Nouwen, Henri J.M. *The Only Necessary Thing*. Crossroad Publishers, 1999.

Nouwen, Henri J.M. *Our Greatest Gift*. Harper San Francisco, 1994.

Nouwen, Henri J.M. *Out of Solitude*. Ave Maria Press, 1974.

Nouwen, Henri J.M. *Reaching Out*. Doubleday, 1975.

Nouwen, Henri J.M. *The Return of the Prodigal Son*. Dartman, Logan, Todd. 1992.

Nouwen, Henri J.M. *Walk With Jesus*. Orbis Books, 1990.

Nouwen, Henri J.M. *The Way of the Heart*. Seabury Press, 1981.

Nouwen, Henri J.M. *With Burning Hearts*. Orbis Books, 1994.

Nouwen, Henri J.M. *With Open Hands*. Ave Maria Press, 1995.

Nouwen, Henri J.M. *The Wounded Healer*. Doubleday,1979.

Oates, Becky. *Grace Stepping*. Cenacle Retreat House, 2004.

O'Connor, Elizabeth. *Letters to Scattered Pilgrims*. Dialogue House Library, 1982.

Peck, Scott. *The Different Drum*. Touchstone-Rockefeller, 1987.

Peterson, Eugene. *Run With the Horses*. IVP, 1983.

Progoff, Ira. *At a Journal Workshop*. Dialogue House Library, 1992.

Rainer, Tristine. *The New Diary*. Houghton Mifflin, 1979.

Richardson, Ronald. *Creating a Healthier Church*. Fortress Press, 1996.

Rutkowski, Todd. *Coming to Life*. VMI Publishers, 2004.

Santa, Thomas M. *Sacred Refuge*. Ave Maria Press, 2005.

Sartan, May. *Journal of Solitude*. Norton and Co., 1992.

Schroeder, Celeste Snowber. *Embodied Prayer.* Triumph Books, 1995.

Shaw, Luci *Life Path*. Multnomah Press, 2004.

Simons, George F. *Keeping Your Personal Journal*. Paulist Press, 1978.

St. Teresa of Avila. *Interior Castle.* Image Books, 1961.

White, James E. *Embracing the Mysterious God*. IVP, 2003.

Willard, Dallas. *The Divine Conspiracy*. Harper San Francisco, 1998.

Willard, Dallas. *Hearing God*. IVP, 1999.

Willard, Dallas. *Renovation of the Heart*. NavPress, 2002.

Willard, Dallas. *The Spirit of the Disciplines*. Harper San Francisco, 1991.

Volkman, Bill. *Basking in His Presence*. Union Life, 1996.

Wiederkehr, Macrina. *Behold Your Life*. Ave Maria Press, 1999.

Wicks, Robert J. *Living a Gentle, Passionate Life*. Paulist Press, 1989.

Wimber, Carol. *John Wimber: The Way It Was*. Hodder and Stoughton, 1999.

Family Spirituality

Boyer, Ernest. *Finding God at Home*. Harper San Francisco, 1992.

Brazo, Carol. *No Ordinary Home*. Multnomah Books, 1995.

Breidenthal, Thomas. *Christian Household.* Cowley
Publications, 1997.

Broyles, Anne. Growing *Together in Love.* Upper Room
Books, 1993.

Erdman, Chris. *Beyond Chaos.* Eerdmans, 1996.

Gaither, Gloria, Dobson, Shirley. *Let's Make a Memory.* Word,
1983.

Good, Phyllis. *Christmas Ideas for Families.* Good Books,
1995.

Lucado, Max. *The Song of the King.* Crossway Books, 1995.

Lucado, Max. *You are So Special.* Crossway Books, 1997.

Lucado, Max. *Because I Love You.* Crossway Books, 1999.

Linn, Dennis, Sheila, Matthew. *Sleeping With Bread.* Paulist
Press, 1995.

Linn, Dennis, Sheila, Matthew. *Remembering Our Home.*
Paulist Press, 1999.

Persky, Margaret M. *Living In God's Time.* Upper Room
Books, 1999.

Thompson, Marjorie. *Family: The Forming Center.* Upper
Room Books, 1989.

Westerhoff, John. *Bringing Up Children in the Christian Faith.*
Winston Press, 1980.

Wolfe, Suzanne. *Books that Build Character.* Touchstone,
1994.

Wright, Wendy. *Sacred Dwelling: A Spirituality of Family.*
Crossroad, 1989.

Christian Psychology

Ashbrook, Tom. *Mansion of the Heart.*
TomAshbrook@crmleaders.org.

Backus, William, Chapian, Marie. *Telling Yourself the Truth.*
Bethany House, 2000.

Brady. Mark. *The Wisdom of Listening.* Wisdom, 2003.

Carder, Dave. *Torn Asunder & Torn Asunder Workbook.*
Moody, 2001.

Carter, Les, Minirith, Frank. *The Worry Workbook.* Thomas
Nelson, 2001.

Chapman, Gary. *The Five Love Languages.* Northfield, 1995.

Chapman, Gary. *The Love Languages of God.* Northfield,
2004.

Clinton, Dr. Tim, Sybcy, Dr. Gary. *Attachments.* Integrity,
2002.

Cloud, Henry, Townsend, John. *How People Grow.*
Zondervan, 2004.

Daniels, David, Price, Virginia. *The Essential Enneagram.*
Harper San Francisco, 2000.

Griffin, Em. *Making Friends.* IVP books, 1987.

Herrington, Creech. *The Leader's Journey.* Jossey-Bass, 2003.

Hunt, Art. *A Weekend with the One You Love.* Multnomah,
1997.

Hurst, Rich. *Intimacy: The Search for Significance.* Cook,
1997.

James & Friedman. *The Grief Recovery Handbook.* Collins,
1998.

Langburg, Diane. *On the Threshold of Hope.* Tyndale, 1999.

Maki, Mark & Juliann. *3 CAIR Manuals*. Unpublished, 2004.

McGee, Robert S. *Father Hunger*. Vine Books, 1993.

McGee, Robert S. *The Search for Significance*. Lockman, 1977.

Minirth, Frank, Meier, Paul. *The Stress Factor*. Northfield, 1992.

Mohline, Dick, Jane. *Emotional Wholeness*. Treasure House, 1997.

Neeld, E. *Seven Choices & Pocket Guide*. Grand Central Publishing, 2003.

Olthuis, James H. *The Beautiful Risk*. Zondervan, 2001.

Penner, Clifford, Joyce. *Restoring the Pleasure*. W. Publishing, 1993.

Quick, Daryl. *The Healing Journey For ACOA*. IVP, 1990.

Richardson, R. *Family Ties that Bind*. Self-Counsel Press, 1999.

Riss, Kathryn. *Journey's End*. iUniverse, 2003.

Shaw, Luci. *Life Path*. Regent, 2004.

Sheey, Gail. *The Silent Passage*. Pocket, 1998.

Stoop, David. *You Are What You Think*, 2008.

Sumner, Sarah. *Men and Women in the Church*. IVP, 2003.

Wangerin, Walter Jr. *Mourning into Dancing*. Zondervan, 1996.

Waterhouse, S. *Strength for His People*. Westcliff, 2002.

Westerberg, Granger E. *Good Grief*. Fortress, 1997.

Whiteman, Tom & Verghese, Sam. *Stress Management Workbook*. Zondervan, 1996.

Willingham, Russell. *Breaking Free*. IVP, 1999.

COACHING SAINTS
PUBLICATIONS
WWW.COACHINGSAINTS.COM

Other Books By
Coaching Saints Publications

Prayer as a Place: Spirituality that Transforms
By Charles Bello
(Available in electronic book formats)

Prayer as a Place is an invitation to partner with Christ as he leads the believer into the dark places of his or her own heart. The purpose of this journey is to bring holiness and wholeness to the child of God. With candor and brutal honesty, Pastor Charles Bello shares his own reluctance and then resolve to follow Christ on this inward journey. In sharing his story, readers gain insight into what their own personal journeys may look like. *Prayer as a Place* reads like a road map as it explores the contemporary use of contemplative prayer as a means of following Christ inward.

Recycled Spirituality: Ancient Ways Made New
By Charles Bello
(Available in electronic book formats)

Recycled Spirituality is like browsing through a mysterious, ancient resale shop filled with treasures from the rich heritage of historical Christianity. Many of the ancient spiritual disciplines have continued to be in use for thousands of years—others are being newly rediscovered. These classical disciplines are drawn from our shared Catholic, Orthodox, Protestant, Evangelical and Pentecostal traditions. The purpose of these disciplines is always transformation, renewal and missional living. As Charles writes, "The gift of tradition is meant to be received. The essence of tradition is meant to be rediscovered. And if the practice of a tradition helps form you into the image of Christ, it is meant to be recycled."

Learning to Suffer Well
By Peter Fitch, D.Min
(Available in paperback and electronic book formats)

Learning to Suffer Well is an interactive devotional study designed to help you think through some of the Bible's teaching about how to face suffering in different situations. It is meant to force you to interact with ideas from the Scriptures in such a way that you will be challenged to grow as a Christian in terms of understanding, honesty, behavior, attitude, and level of spiritual maturity.

From the Sanctuary to the Streets: Insights and Adventures in Power Evangelism
By Charles Bello and Brian Blount
(Available in paperback and electronic book formats)

From the Sanctuary to the Streets is a practical guide written to propel the reader into a lifestyle marked by intimacy with God and power evangelism. Through teaching and personal stories, the authors share with humor and honesty their own efforts to embrace the empowering activity of the Holy Spirit. As the authors state, "We are not called to be spiritual recluses or trail blazing burnouts. Rather, we are called to be friends of God who live a life of intimacy and impact as we simply do life with God in a naturally supernatural way."

The Re-Imaging of God
By Dr. Richard Clinton
(Available in paperback and electronic book formats)

In *The Re-Imaging of God*, Richard Clinton takes us on a journey to explore the ways we perceive God. Our image of God affects every aspect of our lives and our leadership. It is paramount that we begin the adventure to understand our images of God and re-image God based on Biblical images of God. Filled with personal examples, thorough study and reflection questions, Clinton guides us in our endeavor to re-image God.

The Christian Leader's Wish List

A Quick Read Book
By Bill Faris, MPC
(Available in paperback and electronic book formats)

The Christian Leaders' Wish List speaks straight to
the hearts of men and women who are fulfilling their call to
a lifestyle of Christian leadership. While every minister faces
unique challenges, many stresses are widely experienced,
and this book addresses six of the most common wishes
leaders express. This concise, useful, and uplifting volume
offers timely encouragement and practical tools in a format
that can be read in about an hour and referred to again and
again as a personal resource. The topics covered in this
book include: I wish I could find stress relief, I wish for some
close relationships, I wish I could prioritize my personal
development, I wish I could thrive through transition, I wish
my marriage and family could be renewed, and I wish I
could run long and finish well.

You can order these books and additional copies of
Pause, Pray, and Play by visiting coachingsaints.com.

CPSIA information can be obtained
at www.ICGtesting.com
Printed in the USA
FSOW04n2013161215
14288FS